D0388541

Praise for **It's Not About the Bra**

"Offers the parents and the coaches of young players sensible advice, advice that was so often forgotten as youth soccer exploded on the American landscape."
—*New York Times*

"Chastain's book will appeal to all parents."
—*San Jose Mercury News*

"Emphasizes teamwork, sportsmanship, leadership and community service."
—*Tampa Tribune*

About **BRANDI CHASTAIN**

Brandi Chastain, a perennial star of women's soccer,
is among the most recognizable and beloved female
athletes in the world.

It's Not About the Bra

Play Hard, Play Fair, and Put the Fun

Back into Competitive Sports

BRANDI CHASTAIN
with Gloria Averbuch

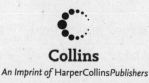

Collins

An Imprint of HarperCollinsPublishers

First Collins edition edition published 2005

Designed by Mary Austin Speaker

Library of Congress Cataloging-in-Publication Data has been applied for.

ISBN-10: 0-06-076600-X   ISBN-13: 978-0-06-076600-9 (pbk.)

05   06   07   08   09   ❖/RRD   10   9   8   7   6   5   4   3   2   1

To my parents, Lark and Roger, who gave me the game,
their support, and, most important, their love

acknowledgments

My thanks to my family, because they are the reason that I started this lifetime quest of soccer excellence; to all my coaches, who at some point saw my potential, and then had the patience to deal with me; to the many wonderful teachers who've lit a fire; to my "little" brother Chad, who played 1 v 1 with me in the hallway; to Cameron, who helps me continue doing what I love every day, which is challenging myself to be a great player and stepmom; to my teammates, (and especially my fellow "91ers," Julie, Mia, Joy, and Lil), who make me realize that greatness comes through hard work, dedication, and laughter; to my agents, John Courtright and Josh Schwartz, for having the courage and vision to dedicate time to a girl who only plays soccer, and who helped give her a face and a voice; to Dr. Michael Dillingham, for putting me back together through multiple surgeries, and to my physical therapist, Ron Kaminski at the MORE clinic, who's motto of "just five more" reminds me that I always have extra to give; to my buddy "Doc" (Dr. Joan Oloff-Solomon), who kept nudging me to write this book; to our editors, David Hirshey, whose passion for the sport has resulted in numerous wonderful soccer books, and Jay Papasan, fellow soccer lover, who helped give birth to this book and his son at the same time; to every young kid I have worked with, or will work with, because they are the future of my passion; to Gloria, because she believes that the game of soccer deserves a platform, and that I am a person who is worthy of spreading the message of teamwork, sportsmanship, and competition. And last but never least, to my husband, Jerry, the coach who all those years ago overcame my stubbornness, broke down my walls, and continues to help me find the best in myself as a player—you're always in my heart and in my mind. I am forever indebted to all of you, because through you I am becoming the person I aspire to be. All my love.

contents

preface: they call me hollywood

They call me Hollywood. I guess my friends and teammates feel the name fits. I was part of that historic day
for American women's soccer, July 10, 1999, when—after
ninety minutes of white-knuckled but scoreless play and
two overtimes—the United States defeated a tough and talented Chinese
team in penalty kicks to win the Women's World Cup. I took the final
penalty kick in that game. You've seen the photo of the moment after: I'm
the one on my knees, my face a mask of excitement and ecstasy, my arms
flexed, my shirt held up in celebration. And yes—I'm wearing a black
sports bra.

How did I know this moment would be so revered? How could I
know that image would make the cover of *Time, Newsweek, Sports Illustrated*, and countless newspapers across the country; that eventually I'd be
seen jumping for joy on a box of Wheaties next to that famous "The
Breakfast of Champions" slogan; that I'd mix it up on *Late Night with David
Letterman*, participate in game shows like *Jeopardy*, or become a commen-
tator on television sports? Who could have imagined all of this?

The truth is I've had the name Hollywood longer than I've had
that sports bra. I got the nickname in 1996, when our press officer, Aaron
Heifetz, was asking my teammate Julie Foudy questions for her team bio.
Under the category of "favorite actress," Julie listed: Brandi Chastain.

"What are you talking about?" everyone asked her. "You know, everything is so dramatic with Brandi. She's so Hollywood," she replied.

Foudy, the team's resident comedienne, gives nicknames to everyone and everything—from the car you drive to the house you live in. "It just doesn't feel right without a name," she says. Mia Hamm, the highest goal scorer in the history of professional soccer, has become "Booter," while hard-nosed defender Joy Fawcett now answers to the uncharacteristically sweet handle of "Joyful." Most recently, Foudy christened our Olympic residency "Villa Viejas" (house of the old ladies). Whatever you call it, this little home is where the veteran National Team players are living as we prepare for the 2004 Games. In a small bit of payback, we call Julie "Loudy" Foudy.

Does Hollywood define me? I guess it does. I like to think it goes without saying that I take pride in the technical aspects of the game, in my ability to finesse a ball through the midfield, bend a free kick on goal, back heel a pass to a teammate on the run, or even clear a dangerous ball from the back line with a bicycle kick. But more to the point, I like to play the game with flair. I try to put the "act" back in action, you might say. So, especially after my genuine but now notorious celebration, the nickname is likely to stick.

If you think about it, there is a little Hollywood built into the game of soccer. The playacting that goes into dramatizing a foul or playing innocent when you're the one who did the fouling is part gamesmanship. And then there's the "never let them see you sweat" aspect that's a feature of all competition. When you're down late in the game or have just made a major goof, you have to act strong so that in the eyes of your teammates, you are a warrior. Then, they can draw from your strength and you can take from theirs. And as nervous as you may be, you try never to give another player, especially the opposition, the impression of your doubt.

That was a prominent thought for me on the day of that Women's World Cup final. When it came my turn at that PK (penalty kick) spot, I didn't want to let the Chinese goalkeeper, Gao Hong, feel she had one up on me. She had psyched me out earlier in the year in a game when I looked up before taking a penalty kick and caught her eye;

meeting her gaze rattled me and my shot dinged off the crossbar. We ended up losing that game 2–1. Not this time.

At the end of that scoreless World Cup final, when the whole team walked to the center circle before the five people from each team were chosen to take the penalty kicks, we were physically and emotionally exhausted, having played 120 minutes of soccer in the intense sun. In the break before the PKs, we wore iced towels on our heads and stretched to keep our legs from seizing up from dehydration. On the field there was no breeze, no relief—the Rose Bowl was like an oversized oven. I remember my feet felt as if they had actually melted into my cleats. I kept a brave face, praying that when it was my turn, I wouldn't go into spasm.

I didn't even know what number kicker I was. As one after the other of my teammates took her turn, I clicked off the numbers. Okay, I'm not number one, two, or three. Then the fourth player went, so I realized, Fine, I'm last.

As I stood awaiting my turn, I shook off as much of my anxiety as I could. This was just like practice, I told myself. I thought of the countless penalty kicks I'd taken in practice sessions, after our goalkeepers were retired for the day, when Michelle Akers and I would keep on shooting on our equipment manager, Dainis Kalnins. But facing the Chinese keeper, I made one small adjustment; unlike my last encounter with her, there was no way I'd look her in the eyes again. My confidence got a boost when Briana Scurry, our goalkeeper, blocked the third Chinese penalty kick. That meant my shot could win the game. If I missed, we'd face another round of penalty kicks instead of defeat. I let out a deep breath and felt as calm and still inside as the amazing quiet that blanketed the more than ninety thousand people in the stadium for this final kick.

A penalty kick is as much a mental challenge as a physical one. The shooter is only twelve yards out and has such an advantage that the keeper rarely has time to react to a well-struck ball. As often as not, the keeper watches the shooter's footwork; makes an educated guess as to whether she is shooting left, right, or center; and commits just as the shot is taken. No one really expects a keeper to save a PK, so she has nothing to lose. All the mental pressure weighs on the shooter.

As I stepped forward, my fatigue fell away. My adrenaline had finally kicked in, and I felt refreshed. The coaches had asked me to take the shot with my left foot, something they had seen me do countless times in training. Just like all the other ones, I repeated, gathering confidence. Just keep the ball low.

The whistle blew.

Jerry, my college coach and now my husband, always taught me that when the best goal scorers in the world shoot, they make as little movement as possible. I cleared my mind, took a short run up to the ball, and planted. I drove the shot with my instep. Shooting it this way, off my laces instead of the side of my foot, was a strategic trade-off of power over placement. If I hit the ball solidly I knew that—even if the goalkeeper got a hand on it—it would still have a chance to go into the net.

I don't even think the ball spun. A near perfect, center-struck ball—it simply knuckled toward the goal. And I knew it was going in. It's like a baseball player who hits a home run and barely feels the effort, because he strikes it so sweet. Gao Hong never really had a chance as the ball rocketed past her into the side net. When I see it now, I think: That was a little too close to the post for comfort!

Suddenly, there was chaos; my teammates sprinted across the field, energized by our victory. They moved so quickly it was as if they'd been resting all day. The fans went crazy. It was a perfect moment. All the excitement, the thrill, and the satisfaction were the culmination of everything that had built up for the over twenty years I had been playing the game. If you're lucky, a moment like this happens once in your lifetime, and when it does, your response can only be uncalculated. So while forty million watched on television and in front of over ninety thousand people (including the President of the United States) at the Rose Bowl, I took my shirt off.

It was spontaneous. It made me notorious. It was not the sort of thing anybody expected a woman athlete to do.

But it's worth remembering that taking off one's jersey to celebrate a goal is common in men's soccer at all levels, all over the world. I guess this was a first for women, as was having an event, and a final, of this magnitude. It became a topic of national conversation. People still ask me, "Did you plan it?" This one always makes me laugh. My sarcastic response is, "Yeah, I knew we'd play to a 0–0 tie after one hundred twenty minutes, during which Lil would clear a ball off the line; it would be one hundred twenty degrees on the field; Bri would make a save on the third kick; we'd be perfect from the spot; and I'd be the last kicker and I would be in the spotlight." Hey, they don't call me Hollywood for nothing.

But in the end, it was just a moment, a celebration. At that instant, as I lifted my shirt, it was as if I'd shed the weight of the entire tournament and replaced it with the thrill of victory and fulfillment at the same time. When you've dedicated your entire life to something, as I have to soccer, and your biggest win comes together so perfectly, and in the biggest imaginable arena, you can't possibly predict how you will react.

It's all history now. And it's pulling off my shirt in celebration for which I'm most known. Does it bother me? Not really. It was obviously a wonderful moment, but I do wish more attention could be paid to the many other things my team and I have done. They add up to a lot more than that penalty kick celebration.

I wasn't alone in achieving fame. We had all been fighting the battle for recognition for women's soccer for so long. Even before the World Cup, this team, and this game, deserved more attention, especially in the United States, where too often women and soccer both are treated as second class. What a burden it had been for Michelle Akers and Mia Hamm, who had been carrying the torch, and were the only prominent faces, for so long. When 1999 happened, it was finally a chance for us to say: This is what we've been talking about all along!

The notoriety that resulted from the World Cup gives me another chance to talk about the game I love, and how it's changed my life and other people's. And now, it gets even better, because I get to do it in this book.

> My objective in writing this book is to issue a "declaration of importance" to parents and children about the game of life through soccer. I want to help people find solutions to problems instead of creating them, to discover the reasons to cheer for everyone—including the competition— and, above all, to find the pleasure in participating together.

I have been in love with soccer from the moment I stepped foot onto the field and kicked the ball. Since then, I have sought ways to use the sport to my advantage, mostly in the game of life. I have been successful as often as not, but throughout my journey I have found the greatest satisfaction in my relationships with family, friends, fans, and the soccer community at large.

And the bra? At first, people wanted to buy it. But even though I am very involved in charity, and felt the money could be used for a worthwhile cause, I didn't want anybody assuming I had set it up or done it for money. So, in the end, I decided to keep it. Maybe someday I'll donate it to a museum, when the time is right to put it among the other historical sports memorabilia. In the meantime, I still have that bra. It's sitting in the bottom of my drawer. Actually, I still use it when I run out of clean laundry.

I am very fortunate that I grew up in an environment that helped me to discover the meaning of competitiveness, confidence, risk, sportsmanship, competence, and compassion. I sincerely hope that this book will help readers discover these values for themselves.

Dreams do come true!
Brandi '04

P.S. *And the experience doesn't end with these pages. You can also log onto my official Web site at* www.itsnotaboutthebra.com *to contact me and participate in fun interactive activities tied to the chapters of the book: I look forward to meeting you there.*

introduction: playing for keeps

In the beginning of writing this book, I was in the airport on my way to a game with the U.S. National Team. I passed a newsstand display that stopped me short. There was a June 7, 2004, copy of *U.S. News & World Report* with the cover story: "Fixing Kids' Sports: Why the Fun Is Gone and the Players Are Quitting. What You Can Do."

"Read this, it's unbelievable," I stammered, as I passed it around to the team. It precipitated a lengthy plane-ride discussion. I was shocked, I told my teammates. I couldn't fathom that adults would make such destructive comments to their own children as those attributed in the article, which opens with fathers telling their kids, "I'm gonna get you tonight because you let me down, buddy," or worse, "You little %$#@&, you could never get anything right." I found it so unbelievable, I had to read it over. No way, I thought, would any responsible adult use sports for such a reward or punishment.

My veteran teammates were equally flabbergasted. Then I came to Abby Wambach, a decade my junior, and thus a member of "the younger generation." "Yeah, I've seen parents go crazy," she confirmed. And Kate Markgraf (Sobrero) chimed in with stories of insane hockey parents she had seen growing up in Michigan.

I mailed the article, which was to be a driving force for this book, to Gloria, my coauthor, with the simple note, "Here's our problem. Let's find the solution."

The horror stories of bad behavior and violence in sports are legion. Some involve just foul language, or a fist here and there. Others are much more chilling. In October 2003, a fifty-year-old New Jersey soccer referee with seven years of officiating experience was slugged in the head and neck by a Clayton High School player after ejecting him. The player was arrested and charged with aggravated assault. Just months before, five players and a spectator were charged with beating a referee following a men's basketball league game in Broken Arrow, Oklahoma. All six allegedly struck the referee on the head several times, pushed him to the ground, and kicked him about the head and body "with force and violence," police records report.

Or consider the Albuquerque, New Mexico, dentist who in 1996 sharpened the face guard of his son's football helmet so he could slash opposing players. Five players and a referee were hurt, and the father was sentenced to two days in jail and community service.

And then, the worst of all. In July 2000, a Reading, Massachusetts, man, Thomas Junta, upset at rough play at his son's youth hockey practice, beat to death Michael Costin, a single father of four, resulting in a conviction of manslaughter and six to ten years in jail.

You would think that death would be enough to alert us all to the sobering reality that some behavior surrounding youth sports is way out of hand, but judging by the continuing onslaught of shocking tales, it hasn't seemed to make much difference.

According to Fred Engh, the founder of the National Alliance for Youth Sports—a Florida-based organization that trains adult volunteers for youth sports teams and has certified more than two million coaches—violence is increasingly prevalent in youth sports. In a survey by the National Association of Sports Officials, 66 percent of respondents from sixty high school athletic associations said increased spectator interference—which often includes attacks on referees—is causing many officials to quit.

Kids may commit some of the crimes, but adults, especially high-profile athletes, set the examples. Whether it's the celebrated case of Olympic ice-skater Tonya Harding trying to do away with her competition, Nancy Kerrigan, in 1994 by having her ex-husband club her on the knee with a lead pipe (a spectacle that made the cover of *Time* magazine); the NBA's infamous 1979 incident when Rudy Tomjanovich, rushing to the aid of a teammate, was punched so hard by an opposing player, Kermit Washington, it shattered Tomjanovich's face and left him lying in a pool of blood; or even the track-and-field drug scandals plaguing the 2004 Olympics—there is an eerie parallel between adult and youth acts of poor sportsmanship and violence.

Consider the similarities of these two: In 2004, Greece's Food Inspection Agency confirmed that bottled water given to players from a visiting soccer team in April had been laced with a powerful psychotropic drug in order to stifle their opponents. In Las Vegas, eight youth football players were poisoned when they drank juice laced with Ipecac; a father had prepared the drink for his twelve year old son to give to a teammate who had picked on him.

The *U.S. News* article credits soccer with creating the real boom in youth sports. After all, it's the fastest-growing youth sport in the country. According to the Sporting Goods Manufacturers Association, the number of "core" soccer participants has climbed from 2.3 million in 1987 to 4.1 million in 2002. All told, 17.6 million Americans play soccer, 70 percent of them between the ages of six and seventeen. And while I would love to be able to say that soccer is an exception to the rule of bad behavior, with its numbers it may, in fact, be one of the primary offenders. I know what goes on all over the country: brawls, fistfights, police summoned to quell arguments—most of them by the parents along the sidelines. The kids follow suit. One African-American boy I heard of had his mixed-race team subjected to racial epithets and other offensive behavior on more than one occasion. And while it seems the vast number of incidents quoted by the media concern boys, in October 2003, a seventeen-year-old female soccer player named Markeya Watson from Maryland was charged with second-degree assault for allegedly punching two players in the heat of a high school game. The mother of one of them claimed her daughter had three teeth knocked loose.

When I was growing up, sports were never very serious. It was really for the physical and social development, the fun, and the family togetherness. Yes, it could get competitive and intense, in terms of our desire to work harder and get better, but I can't recall a single incident of any kind of such violence, or a comment from a parent that could be considered abusive or inflammatory. Sure, one time my dad was red carded and tossed out of the game for disputing a referee's call, but that didn't go beyond the bounds of an overheated coach, or escalate into anything harmful.

Let's not confuse the passion of sports with this epidemic problem of sports rage and violence. Let's not confuse gamesmanship with poor sportsmanship. I put my whole being into the game, and sometimes things heat up. I'll admit, I've gotten into scuffles with players on the field. I'd slide tackle a player, and we'd face off for a moment. But these are not crimes punishable by jail time.

Today, violence and bad behavior in sports is epidemic. Sure, maybe the media does overdramatize some of it, but in highlighting the problem it forces us to raise the question: What can we do to eradicate this type of hostility and negativity that threatens to undermine the games?

I was raised by extraordinary parents, and have been fortunate to have also built a loving family with my teammates on the U.S. National Team. I know that all of them are role models, and that the source of either good or bad behavior lies with those whom we live with, and look up to.

After the passing of my parents, I thought about how much time we spent sharing—as players, as fans, and as coaches. I began to realize that in this country, we're losing our perspective. Sports have become more about winning than about the development of young people—as human beings, not as players.

Competition breeds a type of aggressive behavior. What separates the good from the bad is a person's ability to remember where the line is, and not cross it. I believe that in our competitive zeal we have allowed the positive aspects of sports—most notably, dedication to excellence and competitive drive—to turn into something ugly. In a culture of ambition and rewards, things have simply spiraled out of control. But let's not throw out the good with the bad. Common sense tells us things have run amok, and, while I believe that's true, I resist the message of doom and gloom. The subjects I focus on—sportsmanship, teamwork, honor, learning to bond with coaches and grow stronger from losing—are just a part of what I've gained from the game.

When I'm on the sidelines of my stepson Cameron's games, I sometimes hear parents from various teams yell comments that make me shake my head in disbelief. When that happens, I have the choice we all have: I can blow it off, and hope it doesn't escalate or cause further damage, or I can refuse to tolerate it, and with an appropriate tone, speak up. When I approach the offenders and point out their behavior, they usually react with either self righteousness or embarrassment. Whether they change or not, at least I have raised the red flag. And since this behavior affects everyone, I have made it clear that I don't want those comments to impact other players negatively.

I want to believe there is hope. I know there is. I see it in the many youth clinics I conduct throughout the year. Just last week, we had one of them for inner city kids at the Home Depot Center in California, where the U.S. National Teams train. In a 4 v 4 tournament, two older boys stood out as examples of great athleticism and sportsmanship. They were clearly better than everyone else, but they never displayed any arrogance, and were just as supportive and encouraging to all the players girls and boys, no matter the age. I invited the parents to move down closer to all the kids, and to cheer not just their own, but everyone's children. *This* is the kind of event I wish the media would cover.

I know youth sports can be good—better than good, great. I'm raising a stepson with the same principles that I learned as an athlete, and that I describe in these pages. I believe young people can grow up to be like my National Team mates, every one of whom, I am proud to say, embodies the values that make sports extraordinary and worthwhile.

When I hear people express a longing for the "good old days," I sympathize. As you will read in these pages, I, too, am nostalgic for the simple and abundant pleasures I had growing up as a young athlete. But I also have in mind the vision of the thousands of kids I see in the stands when I play today, and often meet up with after the games, and the many wonderful youngsters I coach in my clinics. I want for them every bit of what I had for myself. We owe it to all of them to make the world of youth sports a better place.

It's Not About the Bra

chapter one: on the ball and off the field

For me, everything in life seems to translate into soccer, and vice versa. It's no wonder. It's my livelihood after all, and I'm also a huge fan. My teammates are my closest friends; my husband coaches collegiate soccer; my stepson is an avid player. When I'm not playing or training, you can find me practicing with my stepson's team, attending games, or watching professional matches on TV. Whether I'm on the field or off, that little round ball with the hexagonal patches is almost always on my mind. Everything I do seems to touch soccer in one way or another.

This goes back to when my grandmother died from cancer when I was ten years old. My mother was an only child, and part of the way my family dealt with the pain of my grandmother's absence was to bond through soccer. My grandfather, who had previously attended games only occasionally, now came to watch me faithfully at all of them, and kept coming until he passed away in 1996, before the first Olympics to host women's soccer. I always felt the family bond when I played.

Having my family in attendance relaxed me, and I often performed better as both a player and a person when they were around. I cherished our time together, and I have always felt great comfort when my family is there to watch me play. That family sports bond is what I try to bring to my relationships with teammates. It's a strong part of the way I approach both the game and my life.

When I step onto the field, my competitiveness gets ratcheted up, and the "warrior" mentality takes hold. Even in practice, all of us on the U.S. National Team are intense about the game. And, when we play, we play to win, leaving it all on the field. But winning cannot come at any and all costs.

Over time, I've come to understand that the player you are on the field mirrors who you are off it. I may go after an opponent in the heat of competition, or even a teammate in practice, but I always try to extend a hand, to help that person back up and encourage her. It's a valuable lesson: The things we do in the course of competition often transcend the moment and reflect who we are. And when they don't, they ought to. That's not something I've always recognized.

But I can guarantee that if you get to know people like my teammates Julie Foudy, Mia Hamm, and Kristine Lilly, you will appreciate the connection between what great competitors they are on the field and the remarkable individuals they are when they step off it. Changing out of our uniforms doesn't change the way we deal with challenges—at least it shouldn't.

When people see our team, they usually see only our success (unless we lose). Even our fans don't usually imagine the hurdles we have overcome to get where we are—as players and as people. For example, during my sophomore year in high school, my team was in a tense semifinal game against the defending champions. I ran onto a long ball sent over the top, and was on a breakaway headed for goal. The opposing goalkeeper saw me coming, but instead of going for the ball, she clotheslined me. She stuck her arm out right across my neck, and I flipped up in the air and landed headfirst. It was pretty ugly. I was the victim of a bad play, and I would always know what that felt like.

Obviously, my opponent stepped over the line. Her reckless, desperate attempt to prevent a goal—which resulted in a penalty kick for our team—could have seriously injured me. Almost every player I know has, at some point or another in her career, employed fouling tactics. Some fouls are harmless, like when a defender gets beat and just latches onto your jersey, knowing she'll be called for the foul and maybe carded. Others are more vicious, like a cleats-up tackle from behind or, in this case, a clothesline that belongs more in a professional wrestling ring than on a soccer field.

The bottom line is, no one's a winner with these kinds of blatant and dangerous fouls. I can understand a jersey grab or shoulder charge, but any time there's a chance of serious bodily harm, that crosses the line. Dangerous fouls ruin the spirit of the game and teach young players the wrong lessons. Ironically, in the end, what the offending player had hoped to prevent often still comes to pass. In the case of that playoff game, our team scored on the penalty, even though I was still too wiped out from being cut down to take the kick myself.

But I have a confession to make. I've not just been on the receiving end: Early on in my career I was the instigator of some dirty play. It embarrasses me to this day to admit that, during my collegiate career at Santa Clara University, I delivered what to this day may be my worst foul. That was a pivotal moment that taught me a lifelong lesson about playing within the rules—whether I'm on or off the field.

I was having one of those games where, as hard as I tried, my efforts weren't translating into much success on the scoreboard. We were dominating, and should have been winning, but we weren't. And my frustration was growing by the minute; every miss-touch and mistake fed my anger. At one point, an opponent took the ball from me, and, like a driver stuck in big-city traffic, I simply went over the edge. In a fit of "sports rage," I didn't care if I went through her to get it back. I chased her down and tackled her from behind, sliding and hitting her midcalf with two feet. I got the ball but fouled her badly in the process.

Half a second later, the whistle blew. Immediately, the referee held the yellow card up to my face, signaling a penalty. According to the rules at that time, that card meant I had to come out of the game.

The card was yellow, but my coach, Jerry Smith, saw nothing but red. He lit into me as soon as I reached the sidelines: "What's gotten into you? That was absolutely uncalled for!" Jerry made an example of me, and my unacceptable behavior, in front of everyone. Turning to me, he continued, "After the game, you will go over and personally apologize to that player and her coach." Little did I realize my humiliation was just beginning.

I was embarrasssed and ashamed. But like a scolded child, I did as I was told. I walked across the field and told the player how sorry I was. Of course, she didn't like what I had done, but she was very mature. She accepted my apology and actually thanked me for it. To this day, I still hold on to the memory of her graciousness. However, when I expressed my regret to the coach, he really let me have it, and right in front of an audience of his players, who were already probably plotting their revenge. "What you did is the most disgusting thing I have ever seen on the field. I can't even believe you came over here."

As much as the player's acceptance of my apology had made me feel better, her coach's reaction made me feel more ashamed.

My punishment wasn't over. Jerry insisted I write a letter of apology to this coach and his team. In the letter, I repeated how incredibly sorry I was for my behavior. I tried to express how I respected the game more than my actions showed. I struggled to explain that what I had done on the field didn't reflect who I really was, and that unfortunately I had just let my emotions take over in the heat of the moment. I wished I could take it back. I couldn't, I concluded, but I swore in the letter (and privately to myself) that I would do my best not to allow it ever to happen again.

While I didn't immediately hear from them, over time we met again, and my mistake wasn't held against me. Later, Jerry brought up the incident to remind the team and me how, despite our desire to win, we shouldn't let our emotions get out of hand. We hope we are forgiven when we make a mistake. But even if we're not, we certainly can learn.

THE GAME OF LIFE

Sports reveal our strengths as well as our weaknesses. Parents, coaches, and peers can help a young player recognize the superhero inside and learn to appreciate her everyday strengths as well. In turn, that person can learn to look inside herself and question her behavior. And it doesn't matter if your game is soccer, basketball, tennis, or ice hockey. The test of your character, the questions, challenges, and lessons are ultimately the same. And so are the rewards we gain from playing the game.

I have found ways to remind myself to maintain integrity in the game. I never put on my uniform until I go into the locker room, because when I pull on that jersey, I focus on the honorable player I intend to be when I go onto the field. That's not to say that I become a different person. But when that jersey goes on, I become a more competitive, aggressive person. While I take on the role of athlete with pride and respect, I also make a point of expressing that side of my personality within the rules of the game.

When you really make a decision—when it's embedded in your heart—you don't have to think about it again. My resolve never to repeat my sophomore-year mistake became so firm it's ingrained. I am very careful about maintaining it—and sticking with the ethics I've learned from my family and my teammates, on the field and off. That discipline takes constant work as well. I'm a very assertive, emotional player, but now, when we have a tough training session where people are tackling, I don't go all out in those tackles. I already know I can go to that place when I need to—in a game, against an opponent—but my instinct now pulls me back from doing it against a teammate in training.

JUST ONE OF THE BOYS by Shannon Boxx

Growing up, all my friends were boys. From four to seven I played on a boy's soccer team. I played baseball with boys until I was fourteen, and from eleven to thirteen, I played on an all-boys flag football team. Being the only girl, I had to stick up for myself and make sure I fit in. If I didn't play tough enough, they were going to tell me, "Hey, you're not good enough to be out here."

When I was young, one of my coaches used to say, "You're always on the ground." That was because I didn't mind being physical, falling, or scraping my knee. So I grew up with that kind of tough mentality. I think that just continued into adulthood. I never even hung out with girls.

Today, I feel as if I am a tough player because of that. I'm not afraid to get into a situation where I might be bumping against someone, but I've never been a dirty player. I've never been one to play outside the spirit of the game. That's just not my mentality. I think that soccer is a fair sport, and I'd never let my emotions get that out of control. Playing with boys, I learned to keep my cool, because if I went out of control with them, I'd get beat up!

I learned to be able to play physical enough to win a ball but not to play outside the rules. I was never taught to do otherwise. Sometimes, I think kids are watching the dirty players. They see a professional slide tackling dangerously, and they learn from that. I don't think I even pulled a player's jersey until I got to college, and then, probably because that's where I started seeing everyone else do it. But now, I don't remember the last time I've even done that. And pulling shirts is the least of anyone's concern. So while I do bring my physicality to every game, I just do it in a fair way.

It's important for a young player to be aggressive and unafraid. I teach kids how to protect themselves—by putting up an arm so they can guard their space, for example. Staying within the spirit of the game and playing tough and aggressive are welcome, and those ideas should be taught and encouraged. But you also have to learn that what happens on the field stays on the field. You can go in hard and tough, and that's fine, but when you go off, that stops. And if something does get out of line on the field, you've got to drop it.

If I'm in a situation where I'm playing for fun, or even in practice with the National Team, yes, I'll go hard, but I'll back down a little bit. I'm not going to risk someone getting hurt. So even if it's a good tackle, I won't do it. There's no point in taking that kind of risk.

I was very nervous and excited to be with the National Team. I'm playing with amazing players. You're always going to be apprehensive at first, but I think what I learned from being the only girl on boys' teams is exactly what I brought to this team. I came here and said, "You know, I have to prove myself. When you're the new kid on the block, you have to gain the respect of your teammates." My first instinct was to do just that. The team welcomed me with open arms. When they do that, it always seems easier to gain your confidence—to simply feel the excitement of being there instead of the dread or the fear. Now, I'm just thrilled to be a part of it.

THE FIELD IS A CLASSROOM

Sports can be a great model for life off the field. Lessons come when we test ourselves on the playing field, and if we're willing to accept challenge and learn from our mistakes, we don't just become stronger and better, we become smarter. Then we can apply this knowledge in other places.

Preparing for the 2004 Olympics, we lived near the Home Depot Center, the training camp for both the U.S. Women's and Men's National Teams. A scrimmage against a national championship Under 17 boys' club team was a test for us. It was yet another example that in soccer, as in life, you are often faced with elements you can't control, and you've got to make the best use of the skills you've been born with. I had no power over the fact that those guys were naturally faster than me, so I was forced to make adjustments to my game. To be successful, I had to be smarter and change my approach to playing. One step was to start talking a lot more with the players who were around me. I removed myself from potentially problematic tackling scenarios by taking an extra few steps to cut a player off, instead of taking him down. (The competition ended up pretty even: We had three thirty-minute scrimmages, each team had a win, and the middle portion was a tie.)

I'm still learning. At a WUSA (Women's United Soccer Association) practice, I was up against Sissi, Katia, and Pretenhia, all amazing ball handlers from Brazil. They have such command of the ball that they make opponents reach and overcommit as they tease and test the defenders' capabilities. That day Katia pushed me to my limit. I felt she was adversely changing the rhythm of the game by holding the ball too long and dribbling too much. Finally, I was just about to go cleats up right through her and let her "feel" my frustration, but I checked that impulse. All a nasty tackle would do was create a negative impression of me as both a teammate and an opponent when I play with the National Team.

Instead of going low, getting down, and lifting my cleats to her to get my message across, I came in with a shoulder-to-shoulder charge and knocked her off the ball, a physical but perfectly professional way of confronting her. It was a legal move that delivered a strong message without hard feelings. And the next time she saw me coming, she passed the ball.

PLAYING TO LEARN

I go to the field every day with the intention of honing some particular aspect of my game, such as 1 v 1 defending. Sometimes, I start the day not knowing which aspect it will be, but it is my objective to discover it. And this is true off the field as well. Every morning during my time with the National Team, for example, I think about something I can do for my roommates living in residency camp that will make their lives a little easier. Making them happy makes me happy. I walk to the newsstand to pick up the paper. I cook breakfast for them or make lasagna for dinner. And I often supply dessert. (Incidentally, that is the way to Julie's heart. Foudy likes her dessert before dinner, or at least on her plate, so she knows no one will take it.)

You as an individual can work hard on your game (and yourself) and you can work together with your teammates. Consider my relationship with Kristine Lilly. We have been on the National Team for over fifteen years. When training is over, or we're given time to work on whatever we choose, Kristine and I may decide to focus on something we've done thousands of times before. In one recent training session, we felt that our angle of approach in taking free kicks was not quite right. Let's change it, we said. We're both potential free-kick takers, but rather than view each other as rivals, we each push the other in creative and friendly competition. We're trying to improve our game and make the team better at the same time.

Kristine and I decide who takes the kick by looking at each other for a sign. I know that she may be the one who feels better at the moment, and she understands it may be me. But at the end of a given practice session, we have both worked toward our particular goal: that whoever takes the kick will be prepared. It's this sort of sharing that is unique to team sports, and it's one of the main reasons I feel they are so great for young players. Sure, I'd love to be the one always taking the kicks, but by choosing to share the challenge and responsibility, I've not only done what's best for my team, I've also deepened my friendship and respect with my teammates. And what's best for the team almost always ends up being what's best for me.

LIFE'S WORK

Team sports such as soccer can also teach us the humility to accept our weaknesses. After all, there's no such thing as a "perfect" soccer player.

Not so long ago, I coached a college player who went on to join the WUSA. When there was extra time, she always worked on her strengths. She never seemed capable of overcoming her weaknesses, particularly shooting with her left foot, because she didn't devote time to them. When things come easily—when you have a specific talent—it's harder to find the determination to work on becoming even better in other areas. It's only natural to savor our abilities, to play to our strengths, so to speak, rather than to work on developing overall greatness. But in the end, when you work only on your obvious talents, you're settling for less than you can be. To become your very best, you've got to own up to your flaws and work hard to improve yourself. Sometimes, players don't have the ability to see these weaknesses for themselves, so if a coach points out a weakness to work on, the player should focus on working to improve it. That willingness to accept and conquer a flaw is something I see in almost all my teammates. They are always exploring their potential, both within and outside of the white lines of the soccer field.

For me, this is more than just talk. When I face painful challenges, I'm motivated by the extra work that comes with them. You may think that your contribution to the game is in how you play, but sometimes you are called upon in a different context. When I broke my foot and couldn't play in the 2003 World Cup, I persevered instead by doing push-ups and conditioning myself. Even with a cast on my leg. I rode my bike on the sideline during training so I could still feel I belonged to the group. I couldn't make the broken bone heal any faster, but I didn't have to sit around feeling sorry for myself. In the process, I also found a way to serve another important role—as a supporter of my team.

I got a postcard after the World Cup from coach April Heinrichs, which said, "Thank you very much for not only being a professional, but for being an example. Your passion for the game at that moment really lifted our team. You could have gotten in the way, emotionally, but you helped the team remember that it's not one person that changes the game.

Everybody together influences the outcome. We really appreciate the way you put the team ahead of yourself."

So pay attention: In sports, as in life, the learning never ends. Just last night in the scrimmage with the National Team, I tackled a male player on a southern California Youth (Under 17) Olympic Development Program (ODP) team, knowing that I had fouled him, but unlike my college incident, it was strategy, and within the bounds of gamesmanship. His teammate made a solid pass; he was making a good run. I knew I couldn't have gotten to the ball, but I also knew he was receiving it at a critical position. He could have gone for a breakaway, so I fouled him to stop that from happening. Yes, the referee called a foul. Yes, I was guilty. But my opponent and I understood. We shook hands, knowing it was all part of the game.

When I do clinics for children, it's a soccer experience, but also a life experience. If I do a demonstration and it doesn't come out right, I tell the kids it's an example of why you should never stop trying to improve yourself. Even as a professional, and a National Team player, I stumble. If I were perfect, I tell them, I would stop playing. We're going to fall short; it's what we do to get up and go forward that will make us better players, and better people.

chapter two: one good service deserves another

My grandfather taught me a wonderful soccer lesson early on. Gayi, as I called him, used to give me $1 for a goal, but $1.50 for an assist. His point was that a goal is great, but it was more important to learn to assist and enjoy being part of someone else's accomplishment. I liked earning that money, especially for the assist, because I could see the pride in my grandfather's eyes. At the time, I also loved watching Little League baseball and I used my "bankroll" to buy candy at the field Snack Shack. My grandfather continued to reward my play right up through college. (Unfortunately, there was no increase for inflation.) He was instrumental in teaching me about other forms of generosity as well. He always supported everyone on the team; if a player didn't have family or friends nearby, he would be that person's loud and enthusiastic surrogate cheerleader.

Today, I tell this story in youth clinics. I tell the kids that great "service" is more than just soccer lingo for a great pass or assist to a teammate. The principle of great service refers to assisting your teammates and community on and off the field alike. It's connected to sharing your time and your gifts with those around you. While I love the game for the physical and mental challenges that it presents me with every day, it's the connection with people that makes soccer so fulfilling.

LOOKING FOR AN OUTLET

My grandfather taught me the importance of unselfish play, but it took a major event to really hammer the lesson home. That was the case for me my freshman year of college at the University of California, Berkeley, when my first major injury sidelined me for the year. Up to that point, I was always a starter; I saw myself as the person my teammates counted on, the goal scorer, the one in charge. I soon learned otherwise.

I had a great run of luck up until that time. Before college, the worst injuries I'd ever endured were twisted ankles and the occasional case of turf toe. An ankle can be wrapped and a stubbed toe can be treated; those things rarely took me out of the game. So, when I tore my anterior cruciate ligament (ACL), I had no idea what to expect. ACL injuries are very common today, but in 1986, no one I knew had ever suffered one. The doctor really had to spell it out for me. He told me that I needed surgery and would then face months of difficult rehabilitation before I could even touch a ball. The treatment back then was a lot more complicated than it is today. Listening to the doctor, I couldn't escape the sinking feeling that my life was about to take a serious turn for the worse.

Today, surgery for an ACL tear is an outpatient procedure requiring only half a day in the hospital. Back then, you had to spend four days. The first time I tried to stand up after the surgery, I nearly collapsed. Dismayed, I realized that I couldn't even get out of bed without help. I couldn't make a short trip down the hall to physical therapy (or to the bathroom) without a hand from my nurse. I'm an independent person, so not having that freedom really shook me. One of the hardest things to grasp was the fact that I would have to rely heavily on other people.

I got through it by focusing on the small, day-to-day victories. When you're healthy, bending your knee doesn't seem like a big deal, but when you're recovering from this surgery, your knee feels as if it's frozen with rust. Moving it two or three degrees is like you've conquered the world. After a lot of work, I went from being able to bend it forty-five degrees to fifty degrees. Later, I improved from fifty to fifty-five degrees. The process was agonizingly slow, but the support I got from my therapists and teammates was remarkable. Whenever I made the slightest progress, they'd cheer me on as if I'd just bicycled a shot into the net.

As soon as I was able, I returned the favor and rooted for my teammates from the sidelines. It was tough to be looking on when I wanted to be that player on the field at the center of all the action. But eventually the injury helped me understand my place on the team. With time, I gained a new perspective on my teammates. The defense; the passes that led up to the attack; the midfielders who stretched the opponent's formation, opening holes for the forwards to exploit—these were things I'd always taken for granted. One player can make a big difference on a team; she can raise her teammates' level, and, sometimes, she can even make the decisive plays. I'd always wanted to be that person, but there on the sidelines I got to see how it truly takes eleven to play.

Snapping that ligament in my knee forced me to acknowledge the roles of the players and our coach, the importance of our fans, and the fact that generosity and sharing, good service and better communication, compose the grease that enables a team to steamroll to victory.

Hardship sharpens our vision, and sometimes it also makes us a bit softer around the edges. The greatest gift I got from that brutal injury was that it forced me to step outside myself. Before, if I had to sit out of the game, I was concerned only with my own role. I couldn't truly see the contributions of others.

About six months before I transferred to Santa Clara University my other ACL tore. My life was about to get tougher. I was a spectator yet again. In one game at the beginning of the season, U.C. Berkeley, my old team, and Santa Clara, my current team, faced off, and I had to sit it out and watch. At the time, Santa Clara, player for player, wasn't as talented as Berkeley, and—believe me—I wanted to be out there helping. But I had already learned I could still support the team. I did it the best way I knew how: I spent the entire game jumping up and down on one leg, cheering. It was probably the only time in my life I was content to be on the sidelines. The best part was that we ended up handing U.C. Berkeley their first-ever defeat at home. And I never even set a foot on the field of play!

As individuals, it's easy to fall into the trap of thinking that sports are all about us, our contributions or our needs on the field. I've seen parents do it, too. They get overly focused on their child and his or her role on the team, because that's their connection to the game. I've learned as a player, a coach, and a stepparent that we're most successful and fulfilled when we focus on the bigger picture—on the value of teammates, coaches, and the rest of the soccer community—from our opponents to our fans—and when we make it our priority to respect one another and everyone involved.

SO MUCH TO GIVE, SO MUCH TO GAIN

Strikers are groomed to be a little selfish, and despite my grandfather's efforts, growing up I took that to heart. Even though no one sat me down and told me, "You need to do it all in your position," or "You need to take the responsibility to score," that was my early mentality. And that attitude got reinforced every time a coach exhorted me from the sidelines to "Go to goal!" or the fans screamed "Take it yourself!" For strikers, that type of encouragement is always around. You hear it so much, you can't help but believe it. It led me to function in a one-dimensional way. I saw myself as a kind of gunslinger on the playground, never realizing how vulnerable I was leaving myself and my team by going it alone. Remember, there is a right time to go "solo," but it needs to be done selectively.

By the time I was thirteen years old, I was intent on being that type of player: Get the ball, go to goal! It took until college for me to truly understand that an attacker should be a defender as well, that all positions are fluid, and that anyone at any given time can be called upon to fill any role. In music, the songs are sweetest when the band is playing together, and on the field, soccer is pretty much the same. It's worth learning this early on; by college, it can be too late. And I believe it's up to the coaches and parents to reinforce this lesson. There's plenty of time for soloists once everybody knows the tune by heart.

In short, if you're blinded by self-interest, you overlook all the other wonderful options that are available. A striker's number-one reward is seeing the ball go into the net. But soccer is a game of many positions and many requirements. In the end, it's the collective effort that counts—how the team played together, not who scored the goal. Anyone can contribute from any position, and all contributions are equally valuable—whether you're making an assist, going for the goal, or cheering your teammates on from the sidelines. As a member of the team, your job is to give your all no matter where you are. When you make a great tackle, or pass, or assist your teammates, the reception from them is where you'll find the glory. Their appreciation and admiration becomes at least as much of a goal as the goal itself. And what's more, on a technical level, having an all-around game means you are a better player by far—never mind all the applications that generosity can have away from the field.

This can and should be reinforced. I talk with my teammates on the National Team about strategy—how, in this game, we often have to change, adapt, and conjure something up in the blink of an eye. Working through any possible situation, in any possible position, challenges us to think about everyone's fluid role, and to open up our perspective. A focus on this kind of thoughtfulness off the field is also a way to connect what we learn from the game to our place in the community at large.

One approach is to let players gain the benefit of playing all positions. As a striker starting out, I didn't especially focus on the people behind me. Today, as a defender, I see everyone in front of me on the field. I have a lot of kids come up to me at clinics and say they've always played forward, and now their coach wants them to play left midfield, or defender. They seem unhappy about it. I say, "You're lucky. It means your coach thinks you're good enough to play in two positions. At some point, everyone is called upon to perform the skills of all positions. Aren't you glad to know your coach has faith you can do them all?"

GIVING AS GOOD AS YOU GET

For me, having a positive impact on others starts with something quite simple: the development of strong character. Sports can help a young girl or boy build self-esteem and confidence. Learning to be part of a team affects how they conduct themselves. They bring those qualities to their school, their family, and their community. Who they become through sports impacts those around them, whether that is intentional or not. Children who gain positive attributes through competition in many cases become leaders by example; people are drawn to them. A sense of self-worth and the ability to share go hand in hand.

Acts of charity ultimately come from being open to others. Sports, especially team sports, have the ability to teach us to be more aware and to respect others. Nonetheless, it's important that parents and adults help set the tone. Giving can begin right at home, or with your soccer team. Coaching, managing, carpooling, taking a turn at snack duty, being part of phone chains—there's a lot to do in any community.

So many examples of generosity were all around me when I was growing up. My dad had a full-time job. But he'd go in to work early to get off in time to take players to soccer practice when their parents couldn't. Three times a week, six of us would pile into our little car (which sat only four) with our gear, soccer balls, and the nets all piled on our laps.

During the time my dad coached my team, we would perform services like organizing community cleanups, or collecting recycling (in the days before it was collected by the city). True, it was to help us raise money for the team, but it was useful to the neighborhood and our education as well. We scoured the neighborhood—picking up newspapers, cans, and bottles—and we had fun doing it. Instead of parents paying all of our soccer-tournament entry fees, we earned some of the money ourselves. In doing so, we learned about the responsibility and value of working to earn something. And we were particularly excited to go to the tournaments, because we had helped create that opportunity, just like a good pass can lead to a goal.

Such lessons learned early can set the tone for later life. For me, those neighborhood cleanups helped shape my work with the WUSA, for example, which translated into an ever-widening pool of do-gooders. During my time with the San Jose CyberRays, I talked publicly about my involvement in various charities. When I would visit another city to play, people would approach me to say that they had heard me speak, and that they wanted to donate to the charity I had mentioned. There are always opportunities to contribute, even for the good of your sport.

THE GIFT THAT KEEPS ON GIVING

Charity is a two-way street. When I do clinics for inner-city youth with other members of my National Team or CyberRays teammates, or when we spend time in children's hospitals visiting critically ill kids, it changes the way we live. We are always a little heavyhearted after these visits. We see the agony of the parents, trying to be upbeat when their children are sick. But later, it's amazing how much inspiration we get from these people's displays of courage and strength.

Some years ago at a hospital visit, I befriended a young soccer player named Casey. When Casey was diagnosed with bone cancer at age twelve, his first question was, "Am I going to be able to play soccer again?" As Casey's physician Dr. Melanie Levin puts it, "His mother was worried for his life; he was worried for his soccer."

When I first met him, Casey was severely ill with a rare form of cancer. All his hair had fallen out from treatments. I winked and told him he looked handsome without hair, and he promised he would send me a lock when it grew back. You could tell he was a fighter. He really touched me, and when I left that hospital, I said to myself, I cannot possibly let anything that I do today in the game get me down. This boy has so much going on, and he is still battling.

Today, Casey is seventeen; he's had recurrences of his disease, and multiple surgeries—but he's a survivor. I'm especially gratified by the fact that his mother told Dr. Levin that she believed a big part of his recovery was the involvement of soccer players from the WUSA. After one of my CyberRays games, Dr. Levin, a Washington Freedom season-ticket holder, approached the fan area and handed me a small box. In it was a lock of Casey's hair, which had grown back after his chemotherapy. I still keep it in my cleat bag for inspiration.

I've shown that "thank you" lock to my stepson Cameron, my husband, my teammates, and my friends. I see it as a symbol of how lucky we can be to have the courage to persevere against horrible odds and succeed—we should never forget that. Casey's lock of hair also reminds me always to share something of myself with others. And I never forget that it is my participation in sports that leads me to important moments like these.

The soccer community has long given me access to people and organizations whose doors would otherwise have remained closed to me. A lot of people seem to listen a little more closely to athletes. I find that amusing sometimes, given how we're just everyday folks for the most part, but at the same time, I've tried my best to take advantage of the opportunity.

Collectively, the players on the National Team have raised hundreds of thousands of dollars for charities. The nature of this team, and of the WUSA, is that if someone needs help, we're there. Whether our cause is professional women's soccer, a community event, or children's cancer research—we're all wholeheartedly involved. And if one person comes up with a cause, we all join her in an effort to support it.

Today, I'm active in several charities, but mostly Children's Cancer Research Fund (CCRF). I'm proud to say I've been the game-show champion of *Jeopardy!* and *Weakest Link,* winning $15,000 and $10,000 respectively, to donate to CCRF. Cancer is very personal, since my grandmother died of it and a close childhood family friend had a son diagnosed with the disease as well. Working toward curing children's illnesses is an especially important issue for me.

There are others who find ways to give, despite the personal and professional demands made on them. My National Team teammate Mia Hamm is a prime example of someone who could easily balk at doing charitable work because people are always asking for something from her. But she doesn't see it that way. Following her brother's death from aplastic anemia, she started the Mia Hamm Foundation in 1999, an organization that raises funds and awareness for bone marrow–transplant patients and their families, as well as develops opportunities for young women to participate in sports. Even without her own foundation, Mia's often pulled in a million directions, with a lot of extended family and other obligations, and although she doesn't have time to do it all, she is as emotionally involved with her work as anyone I've ever seen. I admire Mia's goal-scoring abilities on the field, but I admire her nonsoccer goals just as much.

Volunteerism is a great calling, and the need is everywhere.

Whether it's tutoring young children or visiting a convalescent hospital, contributing on an individual level can be powerful. But for me, it's even better when an entire team gets involved because it strengthens the mission of the group.

ROLE MODELS AND MENTORS

Each individual has an opportunity to contribute in some way, and for those of us who guide young players—be they soccer, basketball, baseball, or football players—that role is particularly critical. Parents, the number-one role models, have a special responsibility to pass on important values and habits, and to help find mentors for themselves (specifically, to help negotiate youth sports) and their children. Young players should also be encouraged to seek out those around them who can act as good role models or teachers. After all, we're all in this together.

I get a steady stream of mail, about two dozen letters a week. I also get a lot of e-mail. I'm pen pals with a few young girls. Sometimes we talk about soccer, and other times we talk about life in general. I met Teresa Rancadore and her family through soccer. She came to a Barnes & Noble calendar signing I did in 2000. Before the event, I had discussed how we all have the ability to help others, and I mentioned my involvement with the CCRF. Teresa showed up at the signing with her piggy bank. She donated everything she had in it to CCRF. Ever since then, we've stayed in touch. She dreams of becoming a goalkeeper at Santa Clara University, my alma mater, and hopes one day to play professional soccer. She was upset when the WUSA folded, and even more so when my parents passed away. Clearly, Teresa gets something from me because she sees me as a role model for soccer, and, I hope, as a person, in general. And from her I get the opportunity to interact with a very honest, open person who allows me to see her pain and her sadness. The very act of reassuring her helped me get past my own disappointment over the end of the WUSA. I also discovered that in talking about my parents, I can honor their memory. When you focus on consoling another, you often comfort yourself as well.

Both my parents were softhearted, and when it comes to connecting with people, my mother remains my shining example. She was a model caregiver, a very busy person who nonetheless always found time to go out of her way for others. From rescuing stray animals to befriending stray people (my mother would often bring strangers to our Cyber-Rays tailgate parties, some of whom, in turn, would eventually become permanent fans), she was truly a proponent of random acts of kindness. And she never quit—she was a full-time giver. She would have been one heck of a midfielder, feeding passes to strikers and helping out the defense whenever she could.

Even after I went pro, my mother set the tone for me. When fan mail started coming in after the World Cup in 1999 and that famous photo brought me notoriety, she insisted we respond to every piece of it. We would sit down on a Sunday and spend four to five hours together. She would open each and every letter and create organized piles according to the nature of the requests.

If I got tired, and those requests seemed endless, she would still insist that they all be met. After a marathon session, I'd moan, "We don't have to do everything." But she would insist that we did. "You have to read this," she would say passionately, "you'll be glad you did." That is just who she always was.

What leads us to give to others? There are a thousand reasons, but the possibility of being a role model is one of them. I go to an event where I'm scheduled to spend two hours, and I end up hanging out for three. Postgame autograph time is fifteen minutes, but I stay until everyone gets a signature. I'm late to rejoin the team, but I feel I have to sign every kid's item. I do this because I've been there. That was me as a child, standing outside the locker room at Spartan Stadium in San Jose waiting for the Earthquakes after a soccer game, hoping for an autograph. Part of me also feels a responsibility to share a connection with the millions of young girls in particular who play soccer, because they are the future of the game. Sometimes, I'll sign an autograph, and a boy or girl will give me theirs back, saying, "Here's mine so you'll have it when I'm famous." I always get a good laugh out of this. If they do get famous, I hope they'll pass on the gift and sign autographs as long as it takes.

Like most very young children, it was hard for me to look outside of my own life at the needs of others. I was a little self-centered at the start, but soccer has been a great teacher. Time, maturity, and good role models have taught me the importance of team contributions, of community service, and of generally just giving back to others.

I want you, the reader, to be involved, too. Perhaps donating to charity and performing community service are already a part of your team and your life. If not, I challenge you to do at least one charitable event or act, and repeat that on a regular basis. It can be through one of the programs listed in the Appendix, or through your school or local organizations. Believe me, it will come back to you!

chapter three: tackling sportsmanship

At a soccer camp I attended when I was eleven years old, Tim Schultz was one of the counselors. Tim played for the San Jose Earthquakes, and I really looked up to him as a professional player. He played both sides of the ball, and I was enamored of his ability to do all the tricks. Every day, my goal was to show him how good I was. In those days, I thought the way to do that was to win. So when my team lost, I got angry. I pouted. I folded my arms and sulked at the far end of the bench. Only about ten girls took part in the camp, and being a girl on the losing team left a particularly awful taste in my mouth. I'd wanted to prove I was as good as any of those boys.

Tim saw me brooding and called me out. "Deal with it," he told me, a flat, unsympathetic response to my lack of sportsmanship. I was thoroughly embarrassed; I admired him so much. Maybe that's why the incident made such a lasting impression. By expressing his disappointment, Tim showed me exactly where he drew the line on behavior. I look back on that day as an early lesson in character development. Now when I am beaten and disappointed and I sense my attitude is heading south, I think to myself, Deal with it, Brandi. Attitude is something we have control over, and that's my cue to regain a more positive frame of mind.

And this kind of attitude transcends the boundaries of play.

Sportsmanship (and sportswomanship) can apply to most areas of everyday life. Being a good sport means that when you are faced with a difficult situation, you play by the rules. When frustrated, you challenge yourself to discover creative ways to take action, rather than descending to the level of the athlete who grabs a headline because of violent or outrageous behavior.

Playing competitive sports provides more than just a way for children to develop as athletes; it also creates an opportunity for them to grow as individuals in their relationships with others—from friends and teammates to parents and coaches. When good values are emphasized, sports can even be a training ground for how to approach the demands of early adulthood—a competitive college atmosphere or first job—or later experiences in a business environment. It can even help when it comes time for players to parent their own children.

SPORTSMANSHIP AND GAMESMANSHIP

I define *sportsmanship* as honoring both the rules and the spirit of competition by respecting your opponent and appreciating the integrity of your team. Without rules, the game breaks down and the joys of competition are lost. Part of the beauty of sport is observing the grace with which athletes react to stressful, challenging physical and emotional conditions. Extract the sportsmanship from the game and something essential is lost. Sports can present chances for improvement, opportunities to learn how to cope better under pressure and to become a better human being. Having a healthy perspective on competition, the kind that great sportsmen and -women exhibit, is one of the best ways I know to get the most out of the game.

When driving, some people see a yellow light and slow down. Others hit the gas. Is it a crime if they make it across the street before the light turns red? It's one of those gray areas that most people interpret for themselves (though I'm pretty sure a traffic cop would have a fairly definite opinion). Soccer is no different. Some fouls are explicitly defined, such as a hand ball in the box. Nevertheless, many referees won't call an "unintentional" hand ball. They don't because of the unwritten standard: Did the ball play her or did she play the ball? For fans and players, this kind of subjective interpretation of the rules is a source of never-ending debate. Is tugging on a shirt a foul or just part of the game? When does a tackle from behind merit a yellow card?

The difference between sportsmanship (or gamesmanship) and bad behavior is found within those gray areas. And it's important to understand the distinction.

While sportsmanship is honoring the written rules, *gamesmanship* is playing the game within its flexible unwritten rules, in a spirit of honest effort, to help you and your team to succeed. Soccer, like many other sports, includes certain behaviors that are part of competition and that illustrate the flexibility of the rules. So using gamesmanship is not necessarily a sign of unsportsmanlike conduct.

In every game, there are legal but crafty ways to gain an advantage: toeing the ball away, for example, or stalling to run down the clock. You're not allowed to elbow a player, but you can lean using your shoulder. There's pushing and pulling, and tugging of the shirt. You get into a hard tackle, and you're knocked over. You put yourself in a situation in which you may get kicked. That's all part of the game. This is the reason that when you're taken down, a thoughtful opponent, one who understands gamesmanship, may extend a hand, which you should take. And if you're the aggressor, you should extend your hand. That gives everyone a chance to catch his or her breath and make sure that there's been no injury. It may even save you from a penalty, if the ref recognizes that no harm was intended.

You learn gamesmanship by observing others, from playing with a good coach, and through playing the game. There are subtleties in play that make soccer very exciting or interesting. Gamesmanship influences how we regard some of these subtleties. Moreover, there should be room for this aspect of the game to develop, especially in young players. Just as some players are crafty when dribbling a ball, there are others who can manipulate a game through savvy psychological gamesmanship. A classic example is the stalling that happens at the end of the game. The team that is behind often gets frantic as the clock ticks down, so you'll sometimes see our goalkeeper Bri take her sweet time as she fetches the ball for a goal kick. Those few extra seconds don't actually change the outcome of the game, but they can derail the opponent by getting her focused on the clock instead of her game plan. Cindy Parlow often dribbles into the corner and just shields the ball until a frantic opponent hacks her down in frustration, or kicks it out for a corner.

Soccer rules are flexible, in part, because referees interpret the game in different ways. The refs are only human (which is worth remembering if you're a parent with a child in a youth league; I, too, have to remember this from time to time). You have to know the parameters of each game; even though the rules don't change, the perspective of the referee does. You can be coached in gamesmanship just like any other aspect of the game, but the most experienced players also learn it by being attentive. In the first five minutes, I have some sense of what kind of game it will be by assessing the referees. It profoundly influences how I will play. I notice if they are calling close, tight fouls. Will they let things go in the attacking third, in defensive third, or in the battleground that is the middle of the field? Or are they touchy, blowing the whistle at the slightest possible infraction? Then, I understand how to tailor my game to give my team the best advantage without inciting the wrath of the officials.

There is an expression that athletes use that is important for fans to remember. Win, lose, or draw, when it comes to what happens on the field, we often say, "It's all in the game." This idea is similar to what Tim meant when he told me to "deal with it." Basically, we should be good sportsmen and -women no matter the intensity of the action, regardless of the outcome. I even try to take that a step further. I believe in supporting and encouraging my opponent. I want the best performance from him or her, not just good sportsmanship, because I understand that a good opponent pushes me to be better, and to elevate my game.

While gamesmanship may have its gray areas, some things are clearly outside even the unwritten rules of the game. Something like head butting, which you sometimes see in professional or even youth matches, is totally unacceptable. Tackling is part of the game, but you should never go at it with harmful intent, nor should a coach or a parent encourage such behavior in any way. Even the away-from-the-body cleats-up tackle is far too often used for intimidation, and, as often as not, a great player is carried off the field on a stretcher. While I would never intentionally set out to injure someone with a tackle, I'm disappointed when my opponents don't try everything possible to play hard and challenge me physically within the lawful bounds of the game. I don't enjoy being tackled from behind, but if someone can cleanly take the ball, I deal with it. It's all in the game.

As a forward, I've been roughed up, illegally and legally. Now, I'm on the other side, and I'm a tough defender, but my intent is never to play dirty. If someone beats me fair and square, I'll be the first to say, "Congratulations." Recently, in a National Team training, Kylie Bivens and I were on opposing 4 v 4 teams. After a long session of hard play and a few rough tackles, we both had differing views on what was fair. We disagreed, and it flared into a heated discussion. But we shook and made up when it was over, and even laughed about it.

Our competitive spirits had gotten out of hand. Everyone loses her cool occasionally, but the measure of the player is in how she deals with those heated exchanges. Kylie and I did the right thing; we apologized to each other and immediately smoothed things over. Accepting personal responsibility is usually a great place to start when you find yourself arguing sportsmanship on the field.

CLASS ACTS

There are certain policies almost every player abides by: You play hard, but you shake hands at the end. When a player goes down hurt and your team has the ball, you kick it out of bounds to stop the play, allowing the other team to take care of their player. You don't ever intentionally hurt someone, no matter how badly she's beaten you on a play. Strictly following these policies defines the behavior of a player or a coach who is called a "class act."

Poor sportsmanship becomes easier to spot when everybody is striving to play fair. When players show they can appropriately deal with the poor sports, losses, and disappointment, spectators and parents should reward this kind of behavior. Unfortunately, this is not always the case. I'm appalled when I hear a spectator or player cry out, "Don't stand for that. . . . Show 'em what you're made of!" These individuals mean to provoke a fight. And that's flat wrong.

In my own household, we obviously talk a lot about soccer. Thankfully, my stepson, Cameron, is very attuned to the fine distinctions of good and bad behavior on and off the field. I'm always pointing out and rewarding instances of good sportsmanship or acceptable gamesmanship. Even if parents aren't very knowledgeable about the game, I think they can still understand general aspects of fair play in their children's sport and engage them in meaningful conversations on the right way to act. Most of the time, to grasp the finer points of gamesmanship, all parents need to do is ask their children to explain what's going on.

Age is not a prerequisite for knowledge, and children who play usually know more than the adults on the sidelines. Parents should take advantage of the opportunity to learn from their kids. Parents can also take the time to talk to the coach or just park their folding chair next to experienced parents who really know the game. I sit with the parents of Cameron's other teammates at games, and we often discuss what's going on. Not that I know everything, but just like players, parents need to find all the most accessible and reliable resources. And if and when you see someone who doesn't seem to quite get it, someone who is encouraging assorted negative tendencies—especially around children—it's worth speaking up. (You should always try to do so in a positive way, of course. I'm not talking about lecturing people.) The whole community will appreciate it.

Sometimes, we forget that sportsmanship needs to be displayed toward teammates as well as opponents. On the U.S. National Team, it's the ultimate competitive situation. We are competing for a limited number of spots, and people's jobs and dreams are on the line. Yet we are constantly reaching out to lift someone up, encourage her, or challenge her in a positive way to be better. Until those cuts are made, we're all on equal footing; and once the roster is selected, that atmosphere of mutual respect is just as important.

How is this kind of supportive team created? Do coaches select players with this trait, or breed this type of mentality? Of course, certain attitudes are to be desired—leadership, creativity, and so forth—so while it takes physical skills to make the team, sportsmanship and a positive attitude are also traits that contribute to a player's survival in the system. And, even better, once you're in an environment like this, it's contagious. You realize how important good sportsmanship is to breeding overall success. Just like one bad apple can spoil a bushel, one tasty orange can spread the sugar to its neighbors—and the juice will be twice as sweet.

The National Team is a microcosm of every other team I've had the pleasure to play on. For all our victories, we've also had our conflicts, and we've shared our darker times.

There are players from the pool not selected for important matches or tournaments, and they suffer just like any youth or rec player who doesn't make it into the game. The best response you can have when you're a disappointed teammate is to offer congratulations to those who made it; when you are selected, remember that it's also important to support those who aren't. When Leslie Osborne wasn't chosen for a recent game against Brazil, I told her, "You're a good player; keep your head up. Use this week away to relax, enjoy a few days, get back into other things, and don't let this be the end of striving for your goals." Julie Foudy said the same to me when I didn't make the roster for Olympic Qualifying in Costa Rica. I can't express my disappointment at being left out, but Julie's encouragement helped me deal with it in a positive way.

Truthfully, it's okay to be upset at times. On the National Team, we have our "bad hair" days just like everyone else. There are times in training when someone kicks a ball in anger or goes in too hard on a tackle. One day, we're teammates, the next, we're on opposing 5 v 5 teams, competing for spots on the National Team roster. But no matter what happens on the soccer field, we never take it into the locker room. Carrying a grudge is a disservice to ourselves and to the team. So when we walk away from the field, the focus is always on remembering that our friendships come first.

These lessons are important not just for players at all levels, but for parents and for the community beyond the world of soccer. I coached a high school soccer team for a year in 1993. High school soccer is light-years away from the National Team. People on that team were participating for a multitude of reasons. Some truly loved the game, while others played because it was a social activity, because a friend was doing it, because their parents wanted them to, or just because they wanted the exercise—all of which is fine. But those who were committed stood out. They came to practice early and stayed late. The others always seemed to have an excuse for their lack of effort. While I'd like to think you can create an atmosphere that stresses team sportsmanship in an environment where there is little cohesion, where even basic commitment is an issue, that can be very difficult. I struggled a bit with that team, as the committed players were continually let down by their teammates.

A lack of commitment can be expressed in many ways: not showing up to practice, being late, having a negative attitude, or being ill prepared to play. And it can be toxic. In team sports, you rely on one another. We recognize that life presents unexpected situations and that we have to forgive our teammates for their occasional lapses, but at any level, if a player makes a habit of being irresponsible or ignoring what needs to get done to solve a problem, that's bad team sportsmanship.

To me, this lack of commitment is very destructive. It's like giving up or, worse, not trying. When this became a problem with the high school team I coached, we had a meeting. I told them, "Look, from this moment forward, we are all going to participate. Even though I like you all, if you decide to leave the team, it doesn't change how I feel about soccer or coaching. I expect the most out of you, so you have to make that decision to expect it from yourselves. If you stay and make the commitment, you show up and put in effort. Your teammates are counting on you." After that speech, the situation greatly improved. I don't credit my speech so much as their realization that they had the power to change their attitudes.

Parents are an integral part of their children's commitment—equal to if not more important than the coaches (at the youth level, at least). They show their support for the team by ensuring the following: that their children arrive on time and are prepared, that they attend practices and games, and that they behave admirably. Parental behavior—the way they cheer their children and other players, as well—is no less an issue of sportsmanship. Positive attitudes and comments are as critical for parents as they are for children, because what young players hear from the sidelines or at home impacts their behavior and can have a lasting influence on them.

While poor sportsmanship can be seen in the blatant disregard for the rules of the game or the safety of other players, I think it is also un-sportsmanlike to conduct yourself inappropriately in other ways. I was taught to have a certain respect for the game and for my team. Putting my-self together and caring for my equipment is as important to me as how hard I play. I not only represent myself, I represent everyone else on my team. I learned this at Santa Clara. To be improperly dressed—with your socks hanging down, your shirt untucked, your shoes dirty—is a sign of disrespect for yourself and your team. On the National Team, we take good care of our equipment. For every game, for example, we are given a kit to polish our shoes before we go out onto the field.

Our keeper Bri Scurry always provides a great model of how this kind of ritual also prepares you for the game. She puts on her headphones and sits on the floor, polishing her cleats. She keeps to herself, and no one bothers her. That's her game preparation. And when you look good, you feel good; you've given yourself that psychological edge to perform better.

PUT YOUR BEST CLEAT FORWARD

Walking the sidelines of youth and professional sports, I see far less civility than I remember growing up. This is not to say that everything was better then. Soccer has never been stronger than it is today, with more kids play-ing than ever before. My concern is that somewhere along the way, as soc-cer has become big business in America, we've forgotten that it is all about having fun.

I have a blast every time I lace up my cleats. I see no reason that every player of every age shouldn't enjoy it as well. We're like a band of sisters on the field, and it's not so different when we've changed out of our uniforms. So whether you play for your school, a rec league, a travel or club team, or even the elite college or pro team, let's all take a deep breath and remember to respect ourselves, our teammates, and the game itself.

How you deal with everything the game presents you with will define how you face challenges in every aspect of your life. So my chal-lenge to you is to put your best cleat forward every time you step on the field.

chapter four: play hard, play fair

I had a rocky start at Santa Clara. I transferred there from the University of California at Berkeley after my sophomore year. At the time, Berkeley was a highly respected, play-off–level team with All-American candidates. Santa Clara was then a decent but unremarkable team with no superstars and no play off experience. I had just come off knee surgery, and when you have a reputation as a player and you're not able to live up to it, it can be tough. I already didn't fit in because I was a transfer student, in a new environment where others had already been established for a while.

When I arrived, few would have described me as a disciplined player. I copped out of running drills, claiming I just couldn't do them with all the training. I couldn't understand how the other players didn't "get it." I was mouthy, disrespectful, and lazy in practice. I certainly didn't give my teammates and coaching staff the attention and respect they were giving me.

Soccer came easy for me, but my fitness level left something to be desired. Because the skills were there, I adopted an "I-don't-need-it" attitude toward conditioning drills. But sometimes an ugly thing happens to even the best player when she's sucking wind—her evil twin emerges. It embarrasses me to say it, but soon my dark side was in full bloom. I complained, deflected accountability for my shortcomings, and generally made a distraction of myself.

All types of behaviors can come out when you're challenged and not prepared for it, especially when you're scared. As a new team member, I felt the pressure to prove I belonged. Unfortunately, I didn't handle that pressure as well as I could have. I was afraid of failing. I had a reputation as a good player, and I didn't want to disappoint anyone. I tried to avoid being judged simply by not participating. I thought that if I didn't try, I wouldn't risk coming up short.

My coach, Jerry Smith, eventually called me into his office. "If you're going to be like that, we don't need you here," he told me, calling me on my attitude. My response was an arrogant, "I don't need you either," and I stormed out. I disappeared for two days. In the end, I came back humbled because I loved soccer and missed it terribly. The long and painful road back from knee surgery had been bearable because I wanted so badly to get back on the field. Within myself, I owned up to my immaturity and acknowledged that I wanted to play for Santa Clara. I needed that positive competitive environment and the support my teammates and coach were prepared to offer.

Jerry took me back on the team, and I turned a corner that day. I played hard, and I also finished all the fitness drills. My attitude was much improved, and as I expressed my renewed commitment in training and games, I think my contributions to the team improved as well.

That's not the only time my emotions got carried away at my new school. I'm like anyone passionately involved in what she does—sometimes I lose control and go over the edge. But as an adult with the benefit of perspective, I can now step outside myself more easily and see the pattern of my emotions. When you're younger, it's much more difficult to analyze and control your feelings. Today, I don't allow myself to react to everything. I believe it's helpful to teach children early on how to handle their emotions so they aren't at risk for becoming the type of players and people who can't understand the importance of self-discipline, both on and off the field.

All too often, adults allow children to behave poorly on the playing field, thinking, "She's just a competitor" or "He's just blowing off steam." But these kinds of rationalizations do nothing for the growing athlete. What youngsters really need is compassionate correction, discipline done with understanding and love. After all, even the best of us slip up. I was fortunate to have wonderful parents who always reined me in, and coaches, like Jerry, who would tolerate none of that kind of foolishness. Even when they were hard on me, they conveyed a strong, important lesson I needed to learn. I firmly believe in a "tough love" approach to bad behavior. While I admit I'm still a work in progress, this approach made a huge difference in my life.

An honorable player is someone with integrity who is also true to herself. Of my U.S. National Team teammates, Cindy Parlow is a good example. At five feet eleven inches, Cindy is a physical presence on the field, and, believe me, she tackles as hard in practice as she does in games. More to the point, she is extremely diligent and honest in her relationships with others. At the same time, she is willing to go completely against the grain, and against popular opinion, to voice her ideas. Sometimes people don't like it, but Cindy has never compromised her integrity or failed to give credit to someone deserving, even an opponent. She's very emotional and passionate about being in the game, and she gives it her all when she plays. But thanks to her high level of sportsmanship, no one who knows her, not even her opponents, would question her character.

While we should battle one another in competitive environments, young players often struggle a lot with separating a person's on-the-field behaviors from the person herself. A player needs to develop the ability to recognize the difference. As I write this, my stepson Cameron's State Cup competition is in progress. As a member of a high school varsity team, he finds himself facing his high school teammates as opponents in club games. He pointed out that some of his teammates were trash-talking. "That's okay," I told him. "They probably just got carried away trying to psych each other out." Still, I know how tough it is to encounter a friend under tense competitive conditions for the first time. That's why, as adults, we are responsible for continually redrawing the lines on and off the field to drive home the difference.

I'm still learning to practice what I preach. The WUSA is an example. When the league began, bringing in so much international talent, suddenly those whom we had competed against for years became our teammates. At first, when Kristine Lilly befriended Dagny Melgren of

Norway, I couldn't believe it. Our national rivalry with Norway is intense, and, as a team, it goes back over two decades. I asked her, "Lil, how can you be friends with her? We don't like Norway; we don't like playing them; we don't want them to win or to be successful." Kristine responded, "You just have to get to know her. You'd love her."

Sure enough, when we were in Portugal for the Algarve Cup in 2004 (an elite international tournament), Dagny came for a visit. It turns out she'd also befriended my roommate Kate Markgraf (Sobrero). Would I have gone out of my way to get to know her? Honestly, no. But as we sat talking and laughing for forty-five minutes, I realized that it's possible to share a friendship with anyone, even your fiercest rival.

THE GAMES PEOPLE PLAY

Good behavior on the field encompasses interactions with everyone a player encounters through the game, and translates into good manners in life. Players should respect both their coaches and their opponents. As with any adult in a position of authority, if a coach is speaking, players should be listening. The idea is to learn from what is being said, and to integrate the concepts of that coach's training, not to complain about not liking that person, or not agreeing with his or her approach. Parents, coaches, and referees should all enjoy similar respect; parents especially should remember that when pacing the sidelines. And thinking that they know better—and are going to make sure everybody else knows it—is not constructive. We all have our individual philosophies when it comes to life and soccer, but I think once players sign on to a team, they have an obligation to do what is being asked of them. That is not to say they can't add their own creativity, their own wrinkle, to the coach's guidelines, only that they need to do so respectfully—and to remember who's boss.

Just the same, players must also learn to respect the role and the judgment of the officials. This is especially important when it seems as if every call is going to the other team. As a player, you have to realize the referee's judgment is never unanimously going to go your way. Just remember they're human and like anybody else—including your coaches, parents, and teammates—they will make some mistakes. Chipping away at them while you run around the field won't win you any calls. It's better to learn from their mistakes just as you learn from your own. The other option may quickly earn you a yellow card and a likely spot on the bench.

I learned this firsthand and it was a bitter pill to swallow. At one point in the WUSA's inaugural season, I had accrued a few yellow cards over the span of a few games. The WUSA rules state that you are allowed a certain number of cards in a given time span. I needed to get through a particular game without a card or face a one-game suspension. I knew that if I could make it through those ninety minutes, my slate would be cleared, and I could begin again. So I was on my best behavior, careful not to say anything to the referee.

At one point, in a bit of gamesmanship, my teammates were illegally stalling over a throw-in, so in an attempt to win favor with the ref and get the ball back into play quickly, I ran over to take it. Instead of penalizing my teammates, who had actually committed the time-stalling offense, the ref gave me a yellow card. I went ballistic: "Do you know what you just did? I wasn't even part of that, so now I have to sit out a game!" (Remember: Do as the teacher says, not as she does! My approach here didn't work.)

Perhaps it goes without saying, but I come from a family of passionate sports folks. My dad was emotional about soccer from day one. He would interject his opinions to the referees. In an ideal world, no matter what an official says or does, you keep your mouth shut. Jerry always reminds me, "You know there are going to be bad calls. You know that at some point you're not going to agree with the ref. So don't be surprised." But even though we should be smart enough to follow that advice and let it go, we all get caught up in the drama. Like me, Mia Hamm is often guilty of talking back to the referee. To her credit, she is almost always going to the ref in defense of another player. Still, I've had a hot temper for all my career, so I strongly recommend that if you have a hot temper, too, the sooner you learn to deal with it, the better off you'll be. And adults—who are often more guilty of this behavior than players, especially at youth games—should be the first to reform themselves.

I see plenty of young players who take the game to heart, and I want to encourage them. However, part of our challenge is to harness any emotional outbursts and use that energy to play. One way to do that is to channel it into physical activity. When you experience a bad call, or a break in the flow of the game, stop thinking about the ref's call and instead focus on what to do next. Ask yourself: How do I get into a better position and get ready for the next play? This doesn't mean you have to agree with the call, but rather that you should get your head back into the game before your opponent takes advantage of your lack of focus.

At this point in my career, I barely hear the commentary from the stands or the sidelines when I play. It's just white noise. In the din of ninety thousand people I focused only on hearing my teammates and my coaches. Players both young and old can learn to filter this noise out. Learn only to hear what's important and beneficial to your game and to let everything else go.

BECOMING A GOOD SPORT

While the ideals of good behavior may come from parents, remember that coaches and other spectators reinforce or undermine those lessons. They can create different atmospheres through their actions—cheering, clapping, yelling—which can influence player attitudes both during and after the game.

Parents have a wonderful opportunity to mold great sportsmen and -women, but there's a lot as well that can undermine the positive influence they have. I can't count how many times I've been to games where parents argue with one another, with the ref, and even with their coach. I hear what some parents on the sideline say to players, and I find myself thinking, How can that possibly help the child, much less the other players and parents? Nothing going on is so important that parents should forget the influence they can have on young minds. By behaving this way they not only embarrass their children and themselves, they do a serious disservice to the game.

My advice to parents: When we talk to our children, let's turn bad habits around. In the game, avoid coaching from the sidelines. Strictly speaking, what kids need is just positive support. The point is to let the kids have fun while they play. What allows that to happen is encouraging vocal support such as "Way to go!" and "Keep up the good work!"

If parents feel the need to advise, they should wait for a break in the action (or better yet, wait until after the game, or wait until the child initiates a conversation about the game) and frame their remarks in a positive, nonjudgmental way: "I saw what you were trying to do. That's a great thought. Is there a way to make that happen? Can your coach, or your teammates, help you?"

Good behavior is also about accepting responsibility for your actions. Jerry insists that his players (and especially Cameron) not take the easy way out. "We lost because we were cheated . . . because the referee was bad . . . because the wind was too strong." These kinds of excuses are not welcome in our house. We always try to turn this around with the question: What could you have done to make a difference under those conditions? We want Cameron to learn to be accountable for the outcomes in his life. The idea is not to make him feel as if every loss is his fault; instead, we want him to learn to look for solutions, for ways he can succeed in any situation rather than for reasons that make failure acceptable.

On the other hand, we reinforce positive behaviors. A high school teammate, the captain who is a senior, made a mistake in a game. Cameron, the youngest member of the team, went over to him and put his hand on the boy's back, and said, "We'll get it right." That impressed me. I reinforced that later by telling him how proud I was. That's leadership in action, I told him.

There are other attitudes when it comes to sports that I think are worth reevaluating. While it isn't my personal response to cry, I don't come down hard on this spontaneous release of emotion. It's simply a natural response to a stressful situation. Crying allows you to experience the emotions of that particular moment, and that shouldn't be stifled. I always think back to that line in *A League of Their Own* when Tom Hanks announces, "There's no crying in baseball!" The gag was funny but really untrue. Take a look at the losing bench after a World Series, and you'll see more than a couple of players with their faces buried in a towel.

Parents raising their voice is one of those borderline behaviors. Leaders sometimes have to shout to make themselves heard, but that's different than parents yelling at their kids. Coaches scream from the sidelines, and teammates holler across the field. I yell at my teammates and they yell at me if one of us needs to regain her focus or position herself differently. But when I yell, it's to dispense information or to elicit a response that will help the team. I especially take care to explain to newcomers that I'm not attacking someone's character.

Young girls in particular tend to take this type of yelling personally, because they are emotionally connected to one another. Boys are generally better at shaking it off. But no one should tolerate teammates who curse at one another or direct verbal abuse at someone who has made a mistake.

I've witnessed "Loudy" Foudy live up to her nickname. The thing that makes Julie a role model is that she's not the kind of leader who would make it personal. Jules is a team captain for a reason: She communicates what her teammates need to hear—be it support, instructions, or constructive criticism—and she's gifted in that her vocal chords can relay that message over almost any amount of background noise!

When my dad was a coach, if a player showed any behavioral problems or poor sportsmanship, he wouldn't tolerate it. "This is not the place for you," he would say, and send someone home. Sometimes I was that someone. I got no slack for being the coach's daughter. My head hung low, I'd walk home red-faced and regretful. The few times it happened are still etched in my memory. I was usually wrong; he was almost always right. And I later came to understand that he was laying an important foundation for my character.

Being a good sport isn't always easy, but straying from the straight and narrow isn't always the end of the world. I certainly tested a few boundaries in my day, and that's okay. In the end, it is up to the player to learn from her mistakes and start making better choices on and off the field. Whenever you make the choice to become a "class act," you'll enjoy the benefits both in the game and in life.

chapter five: champions are made, not born

"When you have your own children, you'll understand."

I used to roll my eyes when my mother would say that. But like parents throughout eternity, she was right. Today, my personal evolution has come full circle. From growing up with my parents and learning the game with them, to becoming a full-time, professional athlete, and, now, to being a wife and parent. And guess what I tell my stepson, Cameron, whom I've known since he was a toddler? "When you have your own children, you'll understand."

It wasn't always such a natural relationship between us, however. Until Cameron was in high school, he lived with his mother, Michelle, about a four-and-a-half-hour drive from us. He would mostly visit his father during summers and holidays, but after Jerry and I married in 1996, we began to talk with him about becoming more a part of our lives. With Michelle's approval, he eventually moved in with us.

The next thing I knew, for the first time since I was a teenager myself, I was fully immersed in the life of a teenage boy.

Cameron's a great kid, but like every other teenager on the planet, he can be difficult at times. Our typical battles include those over his chores. Maybe he tries to get away with straightening the front half of the room to create the illusion of neatness, hoping I won't walk around his bed to see where he's tossed everything on the floor. But he has a huge disadvantage compared to other kids. "Don't try to pull any tricks like this," Jerry tells him, "because I've pulled them all myself."

I care for Cameron as any parent (or stepparent) does for his or her child. I want to make sure he has what he needs. I want to support him in the quest to realize his goals. I also feel a special bond with him because we share a connection through soccer. From the great moments in a game, to the disappointment of being cut from a team, to digging down to find the determination to work harder, he knows I can empathize with him.

My objective as a parent is to help Cameron become the most well-rounded person he can be, to realize his potential, and to enjoy the game each day. In turn, soccer has been a great gateway into his life. It's something we both love and can enjoy together. But it's also a way for us to expand our connection. I'm constantly trying to help him evaluate how to deal with the pressures of the moment, how to understand each situation or encounter, and how to face obstacles off the field in the same way he lets me help him on the field.

IF IT'S NOT ONE THING, IT'S YOUR MOTHER

Another great part of being close to a child who plays soccer is that I can see the game once again through the eyes of a fifteen-year-old. In this way, I get even more out of my sport. I can relive those feelings. With Cameron's permission (I always ask), when I'm home, I join in practice two to three times a week with him and his team. I listen to the coach. I'm one of the players. And of course, I have fun with him. I act goofy and chat up his buddies. I want them to know that even though I'm Cameron's stepmom, I'm also just another player who enjoys coming together to have a good time and play the game I love. As a player, I get an insight into how he handles his sport. As a parent, I get to see him socialize and interact with his friends.

Just knowing Cameron is watching often helps me set the right example on the field. I've been wearing the National Team jersey for a very long time. But, right now, I'm not starting for the team. As tough as that is for me to accept, I know that I have to show Cameron my best side. I have to continue to work hard and help him realize that although these rough times do come, what we do with them is important. I want him to understand that when these times come for him, there is hope and a way to navigate. So, I'm supporting my teammates from the sideline, paying careful attention to the strengths and weaknesses of our team as a whole, and trying to help the National Team be victorious in other ways.

It's useful to realize that you don't have to be a player to parent through playing, and certainly being a player doesn't always make a good parent. My parents weren't Olympic or even professional athletes. They were never on the same sports team at all, but they worked as well together as any two midfielders in the world. In turn, they were great role models for me. They supplemented and balanced each other's strengths and weaknesses with differing personalities and separate backgrounds. And although they were ambitious for me, they were even able to accept that their adult experience didn't necessarily translate for my own needs. Sometimes kids just need to learn for themselves, though parents—myself included—insist that we always know better. Even when we shouldn't. For instance, the day I met the academic adviser for the athletic department at Berkeley, he asked me what I wanted to study. I looked toward my mom. "Don't look at your mom," he said. "You're an adult, and you have to make these choices on your own." I think it hit both of us then that we had reached a new phase in our lives, and although my mom may have been somewhat sad, she nodded her head in affirmation at the adviser's words.

Even so, during a period when I was off the National Team for a couple of years, my mom used to prod me to call the coach to tell him how much I wanted to play, how important it was to me. "That's not me," I told her. "I don't want to call. I'm going to let my actions speak for me." We went back and forth on this for some time, and I finally laid it out for her. "You can want it *for* me, but not *more* than me. It's not yours to want." Even though her intentions were good, she finally came to accept the path I chose to regain my spot, because it was my road to travel.

Looking back, my mom barely got to play sports, maybe a little field hockey, and tennis later in life, so the nuances of playing at a national level escaped her early in my career. But she was very entrenched in her work, and it gave me an example of how to be proud of what you do. She was a businesswoman, but she was able to connect her career to my life in creative ways, relating and comparing even the smallest aspects of her job to my sport. Just as I was the captain of my team, she was the "captain" (vice president, actually) of her business, a temporary-service agency. She spent a lot of time in meetings; I spent a lot of time on the field. Both of us were striving to make our careers run more smoothly.

She understood soccer, because she was around it so much, and I understood her business, because for six months in the late 1980s I put on a suit, panty hose, and high heels and went to work at her company.

Likewise, a great way for parents to understand what their children do is to try it. I'll never forget an all-day soccer outing, highlighted by a player-versus-parents game. My mom was the kind of person who got so involved that when I played, she'd jog up and down the sidelines kicking a phantom ball. That was the extent of her soccer experience. Nevertheless, she still managed to nutmeg me (pass the ball between my legs) in the parent-player game. "And I did it with my left foot!" She told this story of her moment on the field a thousand times. "But you're left-footed," I always teased back.

She was always the person I turned to for comfort and advice when I was injured, or when I was down, having not been selected to a team or named as a starting player. She went to great lengths to make me feel better. That unfaltering support helped me through hard times and instilled in me an invaluable confidence in my ability to succeed.

GROWING UP WITH BRANDI by Cameron Smith

When Brandi took the final penalty kick in 1999, I was in my seat with my eyes closed, praying that she was going to score. I was filled with so much anxiety, thinking how amazing it would be if she made it and how awful it'd be if she missed it. When the ball hit the corner of the net, I just had this huge feeling of relief, that everything I had been hoping for had come true. To this day, people ask me how I feel about it.

I was just a toddler when Brandi played for my dad at Santa Clara. She and my dad got married right before the 1996 Olympics, when I was seven. I got to watch her play. And when I got back to school, everyone was talking about the fact that my stepmom had just won a gold medal on a national soccer team. That's pretty extraordinary, but I was too young to think of it that way. Besides, I've always been used to women's sports, since I had an early introduction through my dad's coaching.

My dad has always felt happy that I love soccer, but if it wasn't what I wanted to do, I also know he wouldn't push me. It's not that I play because my parents do. I play because I love soccer, because I have a passion for the game. They are there to help me if I need it, and they do that all the time.

To me, Brandi was my stepmom first. It just happened to be that she played professional soccer. At the same time, I understood that she was different than other moms, so that made me feel special.

Since I live with her every day, I really don't think of her fame as a big deal like some people do. But it definitely does make me feel proud that she is my stepmom. When I'm asked about the controversy over the bra or magazine photos, I just say there isn't one.

It's just that people don't really know Brandi. She's the type of person who brings out the best in you. I can see both she and her brother Chad got a lot from their parents. The way she was brought up, she won't take no for an answer. I don't want to say she's stubborn, but she'll always push to do her best. She'll go until she can't go anymore. That's something I've always admired in her, and I think I've tried to be like her in terms of her work ethic and being positive.

When Brandi and my dad first watched me play, it was nerve-wracking. We had all just moved in together, and I worried that they might be critiquing me, and that that might influence how they felt about me. But, after a while, I realized they weren't there to watch me as professionals, and understanding that helped me just relax and just have fun. If they are trying to hold back their critique, they certainly hide it well.

They cheer from the sidelines, but they don't yell the way some parents do. They know what it's like for a coach, a player, or a ref to have to listen to that. When I have a question about soccer, or any kind of question, I know I can go to them and they'll have the right answer.

INVOLVEMENT—HOW MUCH IS TOO MUCH?

These days, one of the most commonly asked questions by parents is how much they should be involved and how to express that involvement in their children's activities. Parental involvement is often a source of controversy in youth sports. But, remember, it's not the apathetic parent the media talks about; it's the pushy and misguidedly overambitious parents who make headlines. Not a month goes by that I don't hear about a parent arguing with officials, shouting obscenities, or at their worst, actually starting a fight on the sidelines.

My parents knew that I was talented, but they never crossed that line. When you put kids among their peers, and in a competitive environment, you can see which ones thrive. From an early age, I spent hours on my own with the soccer ball. So my parents knew I was passionate.

Just so, it's easier for parents to fulfill their parenting role when they're on the same page as their children. Parents may love the idea of a sport, may feel invested in their children's achievements, but they can't force their kids to want it—likewise, parents shouldn't fight it when their kids do want to play. In certain ways, Cameron is a lot like I was as a young person. He is also passionate about soccer. Both Jerry and I have been through a lot as players and coaches, and we want him to have positive sports experiences. And yet, just as we have made mistakes, we have to allow him to make his own when necessary. We constantly question what the best approach is to nurturing his interests, without spoiling them. We're particularly sensitive to this since soccer is our profession.

As a professional athlete, on the other hand, I have to be just as sensitive not to push Cameron too hard. In fact, I'm often inclined to back off a little since the assumption is often that Jerry or I would want him to follow in our footsteps. That's Cameron's choice, not ours.

I think the first step in successful parenting is to read young players by watching carefully as they progress. What are the signs that they're content, or that they're overwhelmed? It's also important not only to focus on the difficult or stressful incidents, but to verbally acknowledge when things are going well. Just as good offense benefits from good defense, so criticism needs to be balanced with accolades (sometimes maybe even replaced by them). Too often, we to let the good times go by, taking them for granted. Better to balance focus on the good first, and then the bad. Kids should be told when they have a good game, but the praise becomes meaningless if the child's every move in every game is "great."

On the flip side, there's no point in dwelling on mistakes and lecturing their every misstep. Honest, balanced praise and constructive criticism can help a young person trust and rely on a parent's judgments.

It's not that most children who participate don't want something from the sport—it's just that they may want something different from what their parents want. My advice to parents is simple: Let kids sort it all out on their own.

The most common question by far I get in clinics is from parents who ask, "How do I help my child stick with soccer?" I always answer that I don't encourage any child to stay in something he or she doesn't want. While it's good for young people to experience sports, there is only one way for parents to ensure they will stay with it: Promote and protect a healthy and enjoyable experience, and accept their level of desire. It's easy for well-meaning parents to think they are doing the right thing when they push "just a little bit." There's even this idea that children will benefit more or get over their reluctance or even their "laziness." More often than not, to the child a gentle push feels like a shove.

Just as being an athlete entails some level of creativity, so does being a parent. That said, parents are often much more intensely invested today than they were when I was growing up. There's more at stake now, such as the opportunity to play in higher-level leagues and teams. When I was growing up, the ODP and select teams were in their infancy. Soccer season generally took place in the fall. Now there are endless opportunities for year-round competition and advancement to college, National Team, or perhaps professional careers.

The progress in sports is particularly significant for girls, with opportunities never before available, specifically in collegiate programs promoting soccer. Of the seventy-five universities that had women's soccer when I was in college, few had a full complement of scholarships. Although I was the country's college freshman player of the year, I didn't get a full scholarship until my senior year. Today, thanks in part to Title IX, there are 894 National Collegiate Athletic Association (NCAA) women's soccer programs (294 for Division 1), and there are more women's teams playing college soccer than any other collegiate sport. Those programs, at least in Division 1, can each have up to twelve full scholarships per year to be divided among their players.

But even as the opportunities have grown, so have some of the costs, both financial and social. Parents now pay hundreds, and even thousands of dollars a year for children to participate. Even if they aren't aware of it, I'm sure the cost—both in dollars and hours—of supporting their children's sports career is an underlying factor in parents applying pressure on kids to perform instead of just to have fun.

But the reasons behind the current stress on youth sports don't always reflect such obvious investments of time and money. Our society's fixation on high achievement has invaded the youth sports arena. Parents and players alike put enormous pressure on themselves to succeed. In turn, my message to parents is a simple one: Let's just do our best and extract the good.

Make your priority enjoying the process and your time together. If there is more to come from the experience—some success at a higher level—then that's great, but if all we get is simply being in this healthy environment together, then we are extremely lucky.

Personally, I want to be part of Cameron's soccer life, but I never want to wear out my welcome. He and I can play together, and I can root him on from the sidelines, but we don't always have to talk about the game. There are other aspects of our relationship that need nurturing. I let Cameron decide how much he wants to focus on soccer. That's how I find my balance.

I have absolute love, respect, and gratitude for my parents, but there were times even in my childhood when the balance got tipped. My mom or dad would take it too far. They would yell from the sidelines of a game, and I'd have to say, "Please, be quiet." I remember one time in particular with my Under 12 team, Horizon, which my dad coached. There was no State Cup then, so we were probably playing our local rival. I don't know what was going on in the game, but my dad was on the ref and was also yelling at me. I couldn't concentrate. I felt as if my soccer instincts were guiding me, but every time I heard his voice, I couldn't get anything done. He was trying to help, but it just made me unable to function.

I turned to him in the middle of playing and said, "I can't deal with this." It wasn't that hard to tell him, because I got to a point where I couldn't handle it anymore. I *had* to. He was hurt after I said it, but later, after a brief period of not speaking to each other, I explained it to him: "It's not that I don't want to listen to what you have to say, but at that moment, under the pressure of the game, I was trying to do what I thought I'd been taught in training. But with you yelling at me—I just couldn't think and do."

I felt, and still feel, that if a coach (or a dad/ref/coach in my case) is trying to play the game from the sidelines (i.e., yelling his head off), the player can't make proper choices. The coach wins games in training and, to a lesser extent, in the coaching adjustments that occur before games, during half time, and after the game. Yelling out corrections during the game is humiliating to a young player. It's like the coach is broadcasting that the player's not getting the job done. An older player doesn't appreciate it much either.

With all the time and emotional investment players put into the game, the truth remains that no one gets it perfect all of the time. Overall, I loved having my dad around. He was a great influence on me and helped me become the player I am. I never had to ask him to come to a game. He was there as my team coach from the time I began at eight years old until I was sixteen. Whenever I did play without him, I felt his absence. It didn't hurt my team's success, but I did miss having him there.

I see the parent/child youth sports relationship as a sort of ballroom dance. If one partner is doing the tango and the other is doing the swing, they have no rhythm together. If parents want to be helpful, they have to understand the delicate push and pull between their hopes for their children and the children's own need for independence and unquestioning support. In my opinion, most of the time, you just have to get out of the way and let them dance without you.

RELATIVE TEAMWORK

In addition to the level of involvement, the *nature* of sports involvement in families has changed. The old stereotype was the typical father/son sports bond; yet, the ascent of female soccer has changed that image. With female participation in soccer reaching nearly 50 percent, the strong parent/daughter sports dynamic is a new and refreshing development. And now, dads and moms can not only watch their girls play, they can buy tickets to stadiums to see female sports stars—and potential role models.

It goes without saying that historically families have followed men's sports, like baseball and football. Soccer in this country remains a relative newcomer. Nonetheless, when I was growing up, my family had season tickets to the North American Soccer League's (NASL) San Jose Earthquakes—in my humble opinion, the best men's soccer around. Although I loved going with my parents to see the games, as a girl, I never got to go to a stadium to cheer on the people who most resembled me: young women.

One of reasons the women's professional soccer league, the WUSA, was so important in this country was that, for the first time, soccer dads could share with their daughters what they had traditionally shared with their sons. And as moms got to see athletes who represented them, they gained more understanding of the game and perhaps even more credibility in their children's eyes. Suddenly, parents could relate to both their daughters and sons from a different perspective.

For a variety of reasons—interest, scheduling, or habit—one parent is often more involved in children's sports than the other. But I think it's important for both parents to share an interest, and, as much as possible, to share enthusiasm for the youth sports experience. If parents can attend games together, that's wonderful. It provides a real sense of family. But one parent is better than none; even if one parent has less interest, I encourage that person to consider participating occasionally. The kids will appreciate it.

WINNING FAMILY STRATEGIES

By now perhaps you've observed that each chapter of the book is meant to shed light on some of the practical considerations of the game and on life in general. For parents, appropriate involvement and behavior comes first from understanding the logistics of youth sports. Being informed helps players to play, and helps parents to support their children to the best of their ability.

Practice is a format for training, not just in terms of physical skills, but also for game time strategies. It follows that the game itself should be used to implement the skills and knowledge that grow out of practice. Sometimes, what you've learned in practice you can pull off in a game, and other times you can't, but adults have to remember to let children negotiate their attempts without interfering.

During a game, the coach's job is to use half time to give advice, or to fix, or to tinker with the situation. Sometimes, during the game, the coach feels the need to instruct, but there shouldn't be a constant barrage of advice. And parents or spectators shouldn't undertake any of this coaching job. Parents must trust that their children have gained skill in practice, and that they are trying to actualize what they have learned there in the game. Whether by action (cheering) or simply in attitude, parents should encourage all players, not try to instruct, criticize, or preach to them. I know this is particularly hard, because at times I have had to bite my tongue while Cameron plays.

As players, we all know when we make a mistake (we don't *mean* to pass the ball to the opponent); nobody has to tell us. So parents should think before they speak. They should not jump in with comments or suggestions. Better for them to stand back, wait, and let their children, the players, initiate a conversation. Parents who want to cheer, without coaching or critiquing, should say something noncritical such as, "Go, Lightning." Likewise, comments after a game should be general and positive: "I enjoy watching you. I had a good time."

Baseball star (and Mia's husband) Nomar Garciaparra credits his postgame conversations with his parents as being a major part of his sports (and life) learning experience. "I think the responsibility to educate lies with the parents," he says. "My biggest growth period was on the rides home with my parents after the game. My father would always go over the game. He would ask me, 'How do you think you played?' We would talk about everything that happened, including how I behaved; what was right or wrong. But it was a conversation among all of us, not a lecture. Most important, these talks showed me that, number one, they cared."

Despite the negative images and horror stories we sometimes get from the media, I have no problem encouraging parents to become involved. I hope that with enough direction and understanding, positive intentions will win out. When I was coaching high school or when I coach Santa Clara summer soccer camp, I even invite parents to watch practice. I clearly communicate the rules, however, to both parents and players. It's not just the players who need practice. In turn, I tell the players, "No one is on this field but you. If your parents are here, it's because they are interested in what you're doing, but they aren't going to interfere. They're just trying to learn."

I encourage parents to attend as many games as possible. I go to games—Cameron's and others, like those of my brother Chad and his girlfriend, Erin, who play in a coed league—to see them play. If a child has an issue with a parent's presence, for example, she feels a sense of pressure to perform, or if a parent is concerned about the message his or her presence might send, one option is to watch from afar, where he or she won't be seen (or at least won't be heard). Beyond attending practice and games, I also recommend that they educate themselves. My parents read books, and we learned together. Now, there is so much information, from sports professionals and other experienced families and players, there's no excuse for ignorance. And if they really want an eye-opening experience, they can organize a parent/player game. It doesn't matter to the kids if they're technically able. In fact, it's a chance for them to show off their mastery and to become the teachers. Or, if they're like my mom, the chance to show the players there's still a trick or two to learn.

It may seem like common sense, but it's important to stand back when it's time to stand back. I understand there's an instinctual desire to jump in and help. But a parent must resist, which is something I've learned the hard way. For me, it's often easier to give Cameron the answer instead of letting him go through the discovery process himself. Often I'm not patient enough for him to work through the discovery part, but I've found if he doesn't go through this searching for himself, he won't fully understand or appreciate the answer.

Recently, when he broke his wrist and it was in a cast, I was on my best behavior. I suggested some exercises he could do to stay fit, but I didn't nag him. He chose not to ride a bike or lift weights. When he started playing again, he complained that he was out of shape. Though it was difficult, I refrained from saying "I told you so." Fortunately, he came to that conclusion on his own. He's smart that way.

UNDERSTANDING THE FINAL SCORE

Parent/child relationships are complicated, perhaps even more so in the sporting arena. To the young players I know, I acknowledge that there were times when my parents embarrassed me. But I also loved what they added to my experience. I'm proud of the fact that as my career took off, my mother became the team mom. She held meetings and organized activities and postgame parties. When the U.S. National Team went to the World Championships in China in 1991, she set up an excursion to the Great Wall, and planned happy hours and poker parties played with Chinese money. It gave the other mothers and fathers a sense of belonging, and helped shape the team as a whole.

My parents' involvement impacts my game to this day. I can still hear my mother's cheering voice whenever I step on the field. When I was young, she actually used a megaphone from the sidelines. In the Rose Bowl for the 1999 World Cup final, I could hear my mother's voice ringing out among ninety thousand people. (Believe me, she didn't need a megaphone when I started out, and there were only about a dozen people on the sideline!)

To other parents, I explain that the model they provide, and the lessons they teach, may not seem to be 100 percent appreciated by their children at the moment, but I know from experience that one day they truly will be.

I've had a chance to practice with Cameron, and I hope I remember all this when I have other children, because at some point, I want to extend my family. I talk about it with the other veteran National Team players. We have great role models in our teammates Joy Fawcett and Carla Overbeck for combining career with family and making it work. I think the majority of us want children. For me personally, the biggest conflict is timing, in terms of tournaments and events. I don't see my life slowing down. Like many people, I'm apprehensive and excited about having children. I just hope they will turn out as well balanced and smart as Cameron. With Jerry's and his help, we'll do our best.

WEARING MY PARENTING HAT by Jerry Smith

When Cameron plays soccer, it's important for him to have the opportunity to be the focus of attention—not Brandi or me. I try to keep my distance, so it is his time. It's hard to coach your own child, for him to see a parent as simply a coach giving information. There may be times when Cameron and I argue, the way parents and teens often do. If I were then to coach his team, and that argument spilled over into his soccer environment, it would compromise the place that allows him to be away from the issues at home. It's very important for children to have a place like that.

If I were to be involved with Cameron's team, some players might question him if he were made a captain or a starting player. I've often been asked if I have an interest in coaching women on the national level. Brandi has asked me, and she's confident it would work out fine for her. But I have a hard time imagining this scenario. Although I've been the women's U.S. Under 21 National Team coach, what if I had been involved with the National Team in 1999? What a wonderful moment it was for Brandi to play in the World Cup, and to take that final penalty kick. What if there had been a question about her being chosen to take that kick because I was somehow involved?

Why risk spoiling her experience with that complication? Brandi is a wonderful, passionate soccer player, and just as I don't want to interfere with that, I don't want to interfere with Cameron.

Brandi and I have different opinions on a number of things. We agree to disagree. That's healthy. I'm not sure it's great that she jumps into Cameron's training sessions all the time. She believes this is helpful to both of them. That's between them. I don't get involved because I think I'd be interfering. We're probably both right.

I believe Cameron and I should talk about his soccer, but I do that as his father. I don't need to coach his team or run his training sessions to be able to do that. Just last week we had a conversation. I opened it up: "Let's talk about collegiate soccer, about your soccer goals. Let's talk about your weak areas. Let me help you." It's wonderful that Brandi's dad coached her team, that Aly Wagner's mom coached her, and that Olympian Nikki Serlenga was coached by her mom and stepfather. It worked well for those people, but I don't feel as if it would for me.

I've never been overly involved. I've always felt the need to take a step back. I see so many examples of overinvolved parents. In my determination not to make that mistake, maybe I am overly cautious. My mistake may have been that I have stepped back too far. Now, Cameron has specifically asked me to get more involved. His coach has asked me to help out with the team. He asks me for feedback, but I've told him I'm not very comfortable doing that with Cameron as part of the team.

In the end, we're all products of our environment. There are so many cases of parents who create a situation in which their children are playing for the parents and not for themselves. A number of them have been in my college program, and I certainly see them on the youth level. Players are also fearful of letting their parents down if they quit. Recently, I had to release a player on my team, and the first two words she said to me were "Thank you." She told me she could have never done it by herself. She didn't want to disappoint her parents.

As a coach, I would never train with my players (except for fun, and then it wouldn't be during a time I'd do any coaching). I may get emotional, caught up in playing, thinking about my next move instead of watching the team. I feel that way as a parent. If I'm going to have the luxury of being at Cameron's training sessions, I want to focus on watching him. It's hard to wear the coach's hat when I'm playing, and if I were coaching, it would be hard for me to wear the parenting hat, which I want to wear twenty-four/seven. I think all parents feel this way. I feel bad when I can't have my parenting hat on, for example, when my job takes me away. What makes this all the more complicated is that my job is soccer. When I watch Cameron play, I don't want to wear my job hat.

But how can I not? In many ways it's beneficial to understand the game, but it's a curse as well as a blessing. At times I see too much; at times I'm too critical. I'm very jealous of the parents who don't know anything, and when their child comes off field, all they can say is, "You're so wonderful. You just played your heart out."

Still, sometimes parents with a little bit of information are dangerous. Their child no sooner finishes a game when they immediately start giving advice. What a huge mistake. First of all, they're giving information that is probably inaccurate; second, by giving it, in essence what they are saying to their child is, "You're inadequate. You're letting me down. I need you to be better. Let me tell you how." On my Santa Clara University team, we're trying to win a National Championship, but I don't talk to my players about the game right after they walk off the field. Yet parents, with far less experience, who for the most part probably don't know what they are talking about, give instructions before the game is even ten minutes old.

There's a good reason for this. Parents are very invested, very supportive, and yet we as parents have to be very disciplined. There are so many mistakes to be made. The reason we get it wrong so much of the time is that we love our children, and we are blinded by that love. We love them so much that we want nothing but their happiness and success, and when we see them being unsuccessful, we make the mistake of jumping in and trying to tell them how to succeed. But loving them doesn't make that right. Good intentions still result in mistakes.

That's why I'm jealous of the parents without any information. It's just wonderful to watch them give nothing but support.

I see the other fathers at all the practices, and every one of the games, and sometimes I wish I were more involved than I am. But I'm fairly happy with the balance I've struck. If I were to choose a parenting model, it would be Brandi's parents, Roger and Lark. I know the personal and career sacrifices they made for their children, and all that it meant to them. I see the impact that it had on Brandi. It allowed her to become the person she is.

CREATING A PARENT/CHILD CONTRACT

To be involved, or not to be involved—*how much?* is the question. If parents and players are having a tough time finding a balance, they can consider this novel approach. They can talk things out together, and set some guidelines. If players have feelings about parents' presence or behavior, they should be encouraged to express them. Also, parents should consult each other, as well as experienced individuals outside the family, and continually evaluate their role as children get older, as their goals or needs change, and as they progress to other teams or situations.

To make it concrete, put it in writing. It's really helpful for parents and children to create a formal contract with each other, one that spells out specifically what the child wants, what the parent promises to abide by, and what that parent wants in return from the child. The act of creating this sort of family agreement provides a positive structure to the parent/ child relationship, encourages communication, and nurtures a sense of responsibility and respect for everyone involved.

HELPFUL WEB SITES

www.sportsparenting.org—guidance for parents, coaches, educators, administrators, officials, and all others involved in youth sports

www.MomsTeam.com—a community of parents of children active in sports, all ages and levels; news, practical information, expert advice

www.isoccermom.com—a useful site that bills itself as the Web site for soccer moms, soccer parents, kids, and everyone who likes youth soccer

www.Kidsfirstsoccer.com—a Web page promoting a child-centered approach to the organization and instruction of youth sports

www.positivecoach.org—the Positive Coaching Alliance: workshops and practical tools for coaches, parents, and leaders who operate sports programs

chapter six: for the love of the game

My love affair with soccer began the first day I laced up my cleats and kicked a ball. I was eight years old and playing on my first team, the Quakettes, namesake of the San Jose Earthquakes. A tow-headed blur, I loved everything about the sport: dribbling, kicking, passing, physical confrontation, getting dirty, and running around screaming with my friends. And, the gear was great, too. I was so psyched to put on my white plastic cleats, with the red bottoms and the turned-up toes, the shin guards, the colorful socks, and the jersey. In fact, the first day I got it, I insisted on sleeping in my full Quakettes kit!

During summer, I'd attend the San Jose Earthquakes soccer camps, where the NASL pros served as our coaches. My family and I cheered them on at every game. So I was totally awestruck when the camps started and I was able to commingle with my soccer heroes. All I wanted to do was hang around with them. I carried their shoes for them all around camp. I sat nearest to the coaches' table at lunch, hoping to get one of the professional player jerseys a few select campers were awarded to wear during the week. Okay, so I had a bit of a "soccer crush" on all of them.

I was probably considered the camp brat, because they couldn't get rid of me. And I always wanted their approval. I'd pull off a move and look over toward them with that "Did you see what I just did?" expression on my face.

When the counselors had a two-hour break, they turned on the TV for Bundesliga games. And I was right there with them, watching world-class soccer from the German professional league. I didn't understand a word of the technical terms (it was in British English, and the accent made it tough), but it didn't matter. It was just another outlet for my new soccer addiction, and the San Jose players gave a great running commentary on the matches. One of the things that struck me then was that even these professional players understood they had something to learn from watching the game. Even at my young age, I understood that the first thing to do when we went back on the field was reenact some of the great plays from the match we'd just watched.

If anything, my passion for the game was solidified at San Jose's Spartan Stadium, where I would watch in awe as Earthquake George Best would slalom through a half-dozen defenders to score. (I'll talk more about Best in Chapter 8.) Suffice it to say he was truly a soccer legend. His short but brilliant career still sparks heated debates among fans about his place on the all-time list of soccer greats. Best is probably the reason I started off as a striker and worked so hard to develop a finesse game. Watching him corkscrew bewildered defenders into the ground with his amazing moves and a smile on his face, I said to myself, That's what I want to do. Also, our camp got the opportunity to play in that game at half time, and I scored a goal, and the crowd cheered wildly. In that instant I knew I was meant for soccer.

More than twenty-five years have passed, and my love for the game hasn't slacked one bit. It's my job, my hobby, and even part of my marriage. When Jerry and I finally got married, we were forced to postpone our honeymoon because I was playing in the 1996 Olympics. We waited two years and spent that honeymoon watching the men's World Cup in France. We enjoyed some great champagne and some great soccer. For a soccer nut like me, that's about as romantic as it gets.

I've always gone out of my way for a good game. At the 1994 Men's World Cup in the United States, I drove to one of the games at Stanford University, and on the same day I flew to Los Angeles for another. Just recently, in December 2003, Kristine Lilly and I took a trip to England to watch matches like Manchester United play Chelsea in the Premier

League. Even jet-lagged and sleep-deprived, we sat riveted for every minute of every one of the games we watched.

Soccer is unique among sports in America. While enormous numbers of children play, it hasn't yet seemed to translate into interest on the professional level. The big-money sports—basketball, baseball, football, and golf (mostly men's leagues, it should be noted)—have a huge advantage in that their professional associations have had decades to mature and develop. Until the United States began to do well on an international level, soccer was seen as only a foreign sport. Particularly on the boys' side, kids never had the homegrown heroes they had in those other major sports. Maybe Major League Soccer players like Landon Donovan, DeMarcus Beasley, Bobby Convey, and Freddy Adu—all teenagers when they began playing on the top level—will help change that.

Although there have been some inroads with the men's and women's World Cup successes, the stadiums hosting soccer games are still filled largely with fans waving foreign flags. And those in the South American or European communities in this country have kept their interest separate from mainstream America. Their influence hasn't yet been fully realized on the youth fields that are still predominately populated by white, middle- or upper-class suburban families.

How soccer has become a "middle-class sport" I don't know. One of the reasons the sport is so popular around the world is its extraordinary accessibility. You don't need a special court like basketball. You don't need a bat or glove. All you need is a ball, a little room to kick it, and a designated goal (which I know from personal experience can be anything from a pair of school bags on the ground to an open doorway or even the space between two parked cars). I hope things are changing. I'd love to see the game played more often in urban settings where immigrant communities tend to be concentrated. (In some cases it already is.) Their knowledge and passion for the game would provide a new depth of talent and ability to American soccer.

Recently, I've seen small signs of progress. On Cameron's club team, for example, there are four boys from Bosnia, four of Latino heritage, and one Canadian (he's one of Cameron's best friends, and we always give him grief about being half Canuck). I am also working to bring cultures together as part of a new diversity committee within U.S. Soccer. The aim is to make the sport available to every American community, and to expand the youth game so that it is not just a white, middle-, and upper-class sport. Part of the reason many excellent youth players from other cultures don't participate in organized American youth soccer may be affordability. Youth sports in this country can be exclusive and expensive.

And, of course, I help emphasize gender as a diversity factor. On the women's side, the dearth of players is probably as much cultural as economic. The goal is to convince these cultures to break with a tradition, and to allow and encourage their daughters to play.

"FUTBOL" AROUND THE GLOBE

Jerry says that for me, every day is fan-appreciation day. My birthday presents to Jerry were a satellite dish—"So Brandi could watch more soccer," he says—and TiVo, "So Brandi could record the games." True, I am the embodiment of "fanatic" (in a good way), but I also appreciate the fans who come out to see us. Like those "fanatics," Jerry and I share a passion for being students of the game. When we watch a match—which we do constantly—we're always analyzing every little move. Even Jerry, who is pretty avid, admits he can't live the game twenty-four/seven the way I do. Maybe one day I'll need to join some kind of therapy group to pry me away from the game. "Hi, my name's Brandi, and I'm a soccer fanatic." Somehow, I doubt it will do any good!

As a player, I believe one of the best ways to learn about and improve your game is to plug into the world soccer community. And in the United States, if you don't have a private jet, that means tuning in to games on cable and satellite TV, and following on the Internet. Honestly, things have changed so much from when I was a kid. Back then you were lucky to get a single game a week. Now, dozens of games are broadcast in any given week and almost every major league is represented, from the Premier League in Britain and Serie A in Italy to great South America games in Argentina and Brazil.

I thoroughly enjoy catching the expressions on players' faces when they pull off something a bit cheeky, like a back-heel pass in the run of play. They smile and have that sparkle in their eyes. I love the high fives and the group pile-ons in the corner after a goal, and the samba dancing. I love the personal interactions of the game—both on the field and in the stands—from the guy executing a deft tackle and then helping his opponent up, to the mass of singing fans crowding the aisles.

And to top it off, I love the fact that you can go into an English pub and meet someone you've never met and already have a bond simply because you're both soccer fans. In some American cities that's beginning to happen, too—and that sense of community is one of my favorite aspects of sports.

Also, when you see worldwide soccer at its highest level, the fact that each touch matters, that so much is at stake—like playing an Olympic or World Cup final—makes it all the more exciting. Watching the players work out a problem on the field, realizing the effort that goes into playing, appreciating professionals who are passionate about their work—I can get all of this by being a fan, and every time I watch, I get inspired to do and be so much more in my own game.

For many in the worldwide community, soccer is almost a religion. While in this country we don't yet share this widespread devotion to the game, I see that the seeds have been planted. Even though the MLS is eight years old, it's still in its infancy. The WUSA was also a huge milestone in popularizing the game, so I particularly mourn its demise, at least for now. With luck, we'll be able to bring back the women's professional game before long.

FOUND IN TRANSLATION

I gained firsthand experience of the international scene in 1994 when I played two seasons for Shiroki Serena, a Japanese women's professional team. It was quite an education. Even as the sports culture in Japan becomes increasingly entrenched and popular, Japanese women still suffer from ancient stereotypes. It's radically different from anything I've experienced at home. These women are expected to be obedient, passive, and even submissive, which is not really conducive to rearing a professional female athlete.

I stood out, and not just for my size and golden locks, but because I'm the prototypically empowered American female athlete—vocal, assertive, confident, and perfectly comfortable challenging a player, a coach, the ref, or anyone else. (Even if I sometimes get in trouble.) Let's just say my unorthodox style of play and behavior was a true culture shock. In Japan, if you're red carded, you express your embarrassment by bowing to the stands, and walking slowly off the field.

I never earned a red card, but just as tennis players practice their curtsies before stepping onto the center court at Wimbledon, I learned to respect the habits of my hosts. Despite the many cultural challenges (and the insights that resulted), I managed to be the first non-Japanese player up to that time to receive MVP honors in the league, and made the All-Star team.

Living on my own, negotiating a new country and different culture, learning a new language (which I really miss), and getting to experience the respectful Japanese culture was a life-changing experience for me. I had grown up with imposing myself on the game of soccer, and during those seasons I was forced to be open-minded and to learn how another culture interpreted the game. There were times I didn't agree, or didn't understand a training session. But usually when the cones were placed down, through broken Japanese, a little English, and some international sign language, our team—players and coaches—were able to communicate and make adjustments.

To this day, I feel connected to that experience, and that country. When I hear Japanese, I want to jump into the conversation.

LAYING OUT THE WELCOME MAT, by Marlene Bjornsrud

Not only does Brandi understand the team dynamic, she is always attuned to other cultures. As general manager of the San Jose Cyber-Rays, I witnessed this firsthand during our first season when we welcomed players new to the country. Two of them were the international Brazilian stars, Sissi and Katia. They had never been in the United States, couldn't speak a word of English, and suddenly, here they were coming to play in the WUSA.

This wasn't so simple. Brandi and especially Katia were not exactly friends. They had been rivals on the international scene, and suddenly, they were expected to become teammates. But Brandi's sense of team and community transcended any rivalry.

The day of the Brazilians' arrival is a perfect example of her generosity and team building. She and her mother, Lark, found a Portuguese grocery store, and the two of them worked all day to prepare a home-cooked Brazilian dinner for the two new players. Most Americans would probably have put out hot dogs or hamburgers, but Brandi and Lark welcomed these players by embracing their culture. The message was clear: We accept you; we care for you; you are important to our team. Sissi would tell you that this first impression will stay with her forever. She immediately bonded with Brandi as a teammate, and it set a tone that continued for the life of the team.

In fact, Charmaine Hooper, a top Canadian player on another team, once told me that San Jose was the only team that made the international players truly feel at home. The Australians Julie Murray and Dianne Alagich said the same. I'm sure the other teams did a great job of welcoming their international stars, but having Brandi certainly gave us an edge by comparison. She understands the idea of inclusion and that there is room for everyone. She sees a soccer community that extends beyond borders.

PLAY LIKE A STAR

Loy Urbina has been a soccer coach and teacher in Cape May, New Jersey, for over twenty years. But he was raised in Venezuela and Brazil. Like everyone around him growing up in South America, he was an intense soccer fan. "We would watch teams from all over the world, every day, and then go out to play soccer in the street and imitate what we saw." He points out, "In this country, the only soccer kids know is the soccer they play. Most American kids don't have a team or a player to identify with."

So he tries to give them one. Much like the way coaches encourage young American basketball players to study Michael Jordan, Urbina has created a system for his players to pick a professional team, and an international player, to watch and emulate. "You will be Ashley Cole [Arsenal], number three," he tells a player, for example. He instructs the player to study Cole in action. Players who don't have cable TV have their teammates tape games for them. Then, in practice, he calls out that number to the player as a reminder of what to try. He also brings game tapes of the famous teams for his players and him to watch and discuss together.

So, is your team Real Madrid, or Inter Milan? Is your player Ronaldo of Brazil, Paul Scholes of Manchester United, or Briana Scurry or Aly Wagner of the United States? Your challenge is to pick a team and a player in your position and study them closely. Watch on television or videos (or high-level games in person whenever possible). Make note of what you see. One of the great things about focusing on a player is that you notice how that person maneuvers both on and off the ball to impact the game. Try to imitate something these players do when you play. And never mind whether you're a girl or a boy. "It doesn't matter who you are," Urbina tells his players. "Defenders still have to defend, and forwards still have to put the ball in the net. Look to those who do it the best, and learn from the way they play."

INSIDE THE U.S. NATIONAL TEAM

Like Rome, the American women's soccer community wasn't built in a day. When we first started playing on the women's National Team in 1988, we had perhaps one reporter and a smattering of family members who attended the games. Fast-forward eleven years to the phenomenal 1999 Women's World Cup and consider the difference. That event was the pinnacle of our success: Years of grassroots efforts finally translated into the best-attended, most-watched women's sporting event ever. And the reverberations can still be felt in the women's game.

Recently, we had more than seventeen thousand people come out to watch the National Team in New Mexico, where we had never before played. This was a huge accomplishment, made possible because the U.S. National Team has actively cultivated our fans and always reaches out for even greater connections. Over the years—by word of mouth and through player clinics, autograph signings, and charity events—we have worked hard to make and nurture existing connections. Collectively, our job is not only to improve as individuals or as a team, but also to grow the game of soccer.

The fans are as responsible for that as we are. Our fans and our community are what make this team go. It's their interaction and contribution that also make our sport work. Maybe Jerry's right that every day is fan-appreciation day for me.

RALLYING YOUR LOCAL COMMUNITY

Over the years, soccer has grown so much that it reaches even farther out into a widening community. This is true in almost any youth sport in this country. When I started playing, everything was very local. The Horizon, the team I played for after the Quakettes, was part of the Blossom Valley Soccer League in south San Jose, California. Anyone who lived in my area had to play in that league, and, unlike today, most players lived within walking distance of one other. It was an all-volunteer organization, and the league was far from serious by today's standards. In fact, by the time the next wave of U.S. soccer stars emerged from my area, such as Aly Wagner and Danielle Slaton, they joined a more competitive league.

Today, sports have the potential to take young people much farther afield. And soccer is highly developed in almost every corner of the country. It used to be that the women's National Team was made up primarily of players from soccer-strong communities like California, Texas, or Florida. Now players come from all over the States. My National Team cohort Cat Reddick learned her game growing up in Birmingham, Alabama, and Abby Wambach in Rochester, New York.

No matter where you live, you should know that the game is still growing, and we can all be a part of it. We're breaking down stereotypes about who can play and where. You don't have to be a part of a traditional soccer community. And if one doesn't exist near your home, maybe you can start one—whether in your neighborhood, your junior high, or your high school.

These community teams open up doors to opportunity. In my case, the neighborhood supported me and encouraged me to improve. Although it's not necessarily the reason to play, it's great to get the acknowledgment and respect of your community, like coverage of your team in the newspaper. But the true measure of your soccer community is its value as a place to develop and a springboard for your future.

There are many ways for families to be part of their soccer community, to create this broader soccer "family." Parents can volunteer to be team managers, chaperones at ODP camps, or help on team trips and in area clinics. It's a great way to get involved and give back to the system. (But remember, parents should check with their children, who have to feel comfortable with their taking an active role.) If chaperoning doesn't work out, there are more tasks parents can do behind the scenes, such as phone chains, treasury duties, fund-raising, word processing, and so forth. While these aren't the more glamorous options, they still have to be done.

Young players can share in their community by mentoring younger teams and volunteering to coach in town leagues, youth groups, or for the Police Athletic League (PAL).

Ultimately, you never forget where you came from. No matter where I go, my local soccer community will always remain a part of me. In fact, when I have a break from the National Team, I still play for an amateur team in my area, the Sacramento Storm of the Women's Premier Soccer League, where I began playing in 1990. This was my sole team during the transition in my career after college and when the National Team wasn't practicing.

To this day, I credit the Storm with helping me develop. The Storm helps me keep it real. I feel a great loyalty to Jerry Zanelli, the owner and manager of the team. He afforded me a chance to play during that transition and made me feel I was needed. Without this team, there's a chance I would not have continued to play. Maybe I would have retired. Among my teammates are a number of former WUSA regulars, including Sissi from Brazil, Betsy Barr, and LaKeysia Beene.

chapter seven: there's no "i" in t-e-a-m

Every game, before the whistle blows, I get nervous; it's the good kind of nervousness that comes from being excited and wanting to do well. But as soon as the game begins and I get my first touch on the ball, my jitters disappear, replaced by knowing that I can count on my teammates and they can count on me. We enjoy a comfort level with one another, both on and off the field, that's generated by playing and living together. I've been with some of my teammates so long we've truly become like a second family to one another.

As far back as I can remember, my favorite activities have been those that require the involvement of other people. Everything I did growing up was in groups, from sports to ballet to tap lessons. I've never had as much fun doing something by myself as I've had with my teammates—and that includes enduring the hardest of workouts or the most difficult of games. Even when soccer became more inconvenient—like traveling two hours each way for a two-hour ODP State team practice when I was thirteen—I still loved every chance to be with the team.

My relationship with the U.S. National Team goes back to 1987, when a core group of players, including, among others, Mia Hamm, Kristine Lilly, Julie Foudy, Joy Fawcett, and Carla Overbeck, came together on the soccer field. Because the National Team played only sporadically, it took time to get to know them well.

When we first met, no one was married; no one had children. We hadn't yet shared the experience of going without running water for two days in a hotel in Haiti, visiting an outdoor market in China, or seeing the slums of Brazil. We weren't as open or as willing to give ourselves to others as we are now. But over the years, and especially since 1996 and the Atlanta Olympics, our relationships have really matured as we've played more and more games together, lived through endless residency camps, and played in the WUSA. Imagine it: One day I looked up and realized I'd known these people for basically half my life—no wonder they're like sisters to me.

Just today, I got two e-mails from Julie Foudy. As I work on this book, we are on our break from National Team training camp, and Julie is with her family. "It's really nice being with my nieces and nephews," she wrote, "but I miss you guys the most." A week doesn't go by when I, too, don't wish aloud we could hang out together.

Although I'm friendly with everyone, I'm not saying all the women on the team are best friends. People working in an office don't necessarily love everyone they work with either. It's no different on a team; it just so happens that the National Team members get along extremely well. We know we're going to have to count on one another, so we have a good working relationship. That doesn't mean we all go to dinner or the movies, or live with one another. But there has to be some kind of connection among teammates. Maybe I don't see eye to eye with everyone, or we agree to disagree (you should hear our political debates over breakfast), but I appreciate the strengths each person brings to the team. You have to find a way to make your relationship with others a positive one, and include everyone in the team environment. The tendency is to gravitate to those we are close to, which is okay, as long as we don't exclude anyone.

Being a part of a team means learning to put yourself in each other's cleats. You may see the playing field only from your position, and then, like my fellow defender Kate Markgraf just recently, you're moved up to try left midfield. After that experience, she told Kristine Lilly, who plays there, "Lil, I'll never yell at you to track back again. It's harder than I thought to press forward and then immediately sprint back."

What my National Team teammates and I share goes far beyond soccer, though. It's everything we have faced in life. After my mom died, my teammates automatically came to be with me. The night before the memorial service, Mia, Carla, and Lil flew from the East Coast; Julie and our National Team trainer Sue Hammond made the long drive up from southern California. They went to the store for groceries, and they helped organize the house; more than that, though, they were present and ready to support me in whatever way I needed.

Recently, Briana Scurry's father died after battling many ailments, and everyone mobilized to be there for her. It's understood that this is simply how we are as teammates. And the beauty of team sports is that when you go through something together—whether it's really painful or exciting beyond belief—those shared feelings add new depth to your relationship.

Right before we play, our team captain Julie Foudy always says a few words to unite us. It's not a chalk talk—nothing too long or elaborate—it's just something to create intensity and get us ready. If we're playing Norway, she might say, "Come out hard and deny the long service. We will not be beaten in the air today. It's a bad day to be Norwegian!" She gets us to laugh, which is great for shaking off any pregame nerves. And then, we'll do our team cheer, "USA, USA, USA" but pronounced "uuu-sah, uuu-sah, uuu-sah, ah!" It's the same cheer we've done since I've been on the team. And for me, the sound makes me feel as if we could never lose.

LEARNING TO BE A TEAM PLAYER, by Jerry Smith

In 1989, Brandi's first year at Santa Clara, she was on her own page. We were as blue collar a team as it gets, with no scholarship money. We were never going to be successful without a tremendous amount of hard work by each and every player during that season. Brandi was unfit and using her knee surgery to back out of the physical demands being put on the team. What she didn't understand was that many of those physical demands were designed to challenge the players' mental toughness, not their fitness. In a word, she was failing to meet those challenges.

Ironically, as out of shape as she was, Brandi was the best player on our team in terms of technical and tactical ability and even athleticism. After the coaching staff decided we didn't need her to be a part of our team, and she decided she didn't want to be either, I was surprised to see her walk back into the training session two days later. So I changed what I had planned and made it the most physically demanding session I had ever had. Not only did she finish, she was at the front of the pack in everything we did. Tough love had banished her bad attitude.

I could name a lot of people, and a lot of reasons, for our success, but the way Brandi became a crucial part of that success just fascinates me. We achieved our number-one ranking and a trip to the NCAA tournament that year, thanks largely to Brandi's leadership. She turned things around big time, and set the tone for the whole team.

FROM PATIENT TO PATIENCE

The challenges of being on a team can be like making your way through a maze. When I was just beginning on the National Team, the competition for playing time was cutthroat. If you weren't a starter, you almost never got into a game. In my first two years on this team, I played very few games.

You may find yourself in a situation similar to that—being new to a team, trying to break into an established group of players, hoping to get the coach to notice your abilities, and not feeling as relaxed or at ease as the others. Here's some advice: Be patient. Ride it out. Seek out the veteran members of the group you sense can support you in your adjustment phase. Don't wallow in self-doubt. Be proactive and engage teammates to help you work on your deficiencies. Empower yourself to create a positive change.

At the time I faced these challenges on the National Team, my roommate Wendy Gebauer (now Palladino) and I spent a lot of time together. That relationship was very important to me. She reached out to me and helped me feel I was part of the team. It's so important to feel wanted and needed. Wendy and others like her did that for me. I think that's one of the reasons I now go out of my way to welcome newcomers. After all, the sooner they feel a part of the team, the better you'll all work together when crunch time rolls around.

This translates to a good lesson for youth leagues, too. Teams will have players who are bigger, faster, better, or more dominant; there may be bullies, or insensitive kids. But if players and adults stress team concepts, communication, and hard work, you may have fewer situations in which some players feel left out. From the coach's perspective, it might be a good idea to match a struggling player with the most-skilled and best-liked player.

A few months ago, I did a clinic with about thirty girls and only one boy. You could see the discomfort that boy felt, so I made him my partner. Then, when we got going, I brought a girl in and made it three. When I could see he was comfortable and absorbed in the activity, I was able to leave the two of them.

If you stick around long enough, you even get a chance to reapply the knowledge that you gained through earlier difficulties. In the 2003 World Cup, I broke my foot in the first half of the first game and had to sit out the remainder of the tournament. I had a rough time getting back on the team, and now, as we prepare for the 2004 Olympics, I'm still coming off the bench. I have to tell myself, Okay, this is another chance to test myself, my physical and mental capacity, and my psychological strength. Is it hard? Of course, it's very hard some days, because I feel most of all as if I want to contribute. It's not about getting attention for myself; it's about wanting to help the team. Usually, the way you do that is by playing in the game. But as a veteran, I find myself asking, How will I negotiate this? What kind of relationship will I have with the others who are playing in my position? I already understand the challenges to succeed in the team environment. Everyone wants to play; everyone wants to start. And just because you have achieved something many times doesn't mean you won't have to prove yourself again.

When it rains it pours, as the saying goes, and those challenges we face seem to have a way of compounding themselves. Recently, I hurt my foot for the second time. A million negative thoughts went through my mind as I was driving to the doctor: I can't believe this is happening again and so close to the Olympics. I was just starting to make my way back, and play well. Then, I got some good news: There was no fracture, just a bruise. So, at the Olympic camp, I bring my Pilates ball, elastic bands, and medicine ball to practice and do my exercises from the sideline. The girls give me a shout-out. That's my team, and I'm so grateful I have them.

IMPROVING AND IMPROVISING

Soccer teams have a built-in competitive dynamic, because there is almost always a core group of players who either start or get a lot of playing time. Then, there's another group that works hard but doesn't get into the game. What's difficult is that we all have the desire to get onto the field, but we have to be realists. We can't all play all ninety minutes. We have to find ways to get beyond that obstacle, and to get our validation from our teammates. It helps to learn to take a measure of pride and pleasure in the fact that we are part of the group, and to learn to help the team cause at the same time.

Take it from me: When you're one of those players on the bench, it's easy to feel as if you're not contributing. But remember, you're one of the ones pushing the starting eleven, forcing them to improve and be the best they can be by going against them in training every time out. When we won our first World Cup in 1991, the starters were asked about how they had prepared, and who was the toughest competition they had played against. Their answer was our second team, the nonstarters.

Just the same, everyone should have the opportunity to evolve, but the amazing thing is that on a team, even when you can't see it yourself, that's constantly happening. Only yesterday the team coach, April Heinrichs, called a meeting. She talked about the different players. There are some who are very new to residency camp, who are enjoying their first experience here. There are senior players, in their fifth residency, who know the rules and the flow. Then there are the players coming back to try to reinvent themselves. I went up to April after the meeting and said, "That's me."

I'm that player who is trying every day to get better, savvier. My daily mission is to view the game as if it comes at me in slow motion so I can become a better decision maker. And I try to be open to whatever the coaches ask of me. Right now, they want to try me at different positions. Does that mean I'm not good enough in my current position? Or that I'm so good they want to experiment with me elsewhere? Thirty years and I still don't know the answers! I simply trust that what's best for the team is best for me.

Today, on my way home from the airport, Aly Wagner pointed out, "Oh, it's only eleven days until they name the twenty-two players for the Olympic team." My stomach was in knots. I try to convince myself that maybe the nervousness is a good thing. Maybe it makes me care even more, work even harder. The point is that the game is always new, and always presents a challenge.

CAPPING OFF A CAREER

I reached a huge milestone when I achieved one hundred caps on July 4, 1999, in the World Cup game against Brazil in California, near my home, at Stanford Stadium. (A cap in soccer means you've made an appearance for the National Team. The term originated in England in the 1800s, when, for practical reasons, players were given wool caps for their participation. In our system, after one hundred caps, you are given a watch. I think it would be awesome if they still gave out caps.) I was honored to follow in the footsteps of my teammates who preceded me with one hundred caps, although Lil, Jules, Mia, and Joy would need to make additions to their homes to accommodate all their caps. (Each of them has topped two hundred now!)

That's my goal as well, to break the two-hundred mark.

AMERICAN PLAYERS WITH 100 OR MORE CAPS[*]

	Player	Pos.	Caps
1.	Kristine Lilly	M	277
2.	Mia Hamm	F	261
3.	Julie Foudy	M	257
4.	Joy Fawcett	D	234
5.	Tiffeny Milbrett	F	199
6.	Brandi Chastain	D	179
7.	Shannon MacMillan	M	171
8.	Carla Overbeck	D	168
9.	Michelle Akers	M	153
10.	Cindy Parlow	F	147
11.	Briana Scurry	G	141
12.	Tisha Venturini	M	132
13.	Kate Markgraf	D	122
14.	Christie Rampone	D	122
15.	Carin Gabarra	F	117
16.	Lorrie Fair	D	114
17.	Tiffany Roberts	M	107

*as of August 12, 2004

As much as I appreciate the honor, my hundredth cap also reminds me that even after a person makes a team, there are many other goals to achieve. Even with a gold medal and world championships under my belt, it isn't as if I'm tenured for life. I have to make the team every day through my play and leadership. Other players respect this, because they, too, face the challenge of proving themselves. When a substitute who rarely plays gets to go into a game, even if it's only for ten minutes, she often gets the loudest cheers from the veterans. That's because everyone knows how hard she worked to deserve even a fraction of playing time. And that, too, is an honor.

CONCOCTING BETTER RESULTS THROUGH TEAM CHEMISTRY

It's easy to have good team chemistry when your team is winning. It's when you're losing that you see everyone's true colors. I talk a lot in this book about the National Team and our wonderful connections, but I've also been on teams with poor chemistry.

My first year of high school comes to mind, when I came into a group of established juniors and seniors. Teams like those in high school are often made up of older players who want the team to be successful, but may be ambivalent about a newcomer's success because they don't want the newcomer to take their position. That was my experience that first year. But I still found something to enjoy in my freshman year. I had made the varsity and, even though the senior members made sure we knew we were freshman, they accepted us in the end. I try to hold true to that line when new players come onto the National Team.

All kinds of relationships grow out of the team experience. For me, soccer is where the seeds of family and friendship bear fruit. It's where you learn how to act, how to appreciate and be sensitive to others, and, basically, how to live with other people. If you're lucky, it's also where you first experience team chemistry.

Preparing for the 2004 Olympics, I'm living with Mia, Julie, and Lil. This is the fifth residency camp for them, the fourth for me. Each camp has been a different journey, with different challenges and obstacles we have to plan for, as well as those we don't see until we're right on top of them. Some days, we're not feeling our best, and we need moral support from one another. I think it's that kind of daily support that makes it easier to go forward, especially when it gets difficult—and it does get difficult.

Right now, I'm in an air cast to protect my injured foot. Every day, while I wait for it to heal, I get an e-mail or a phone call from my teammates asking how I'm doing. When we're not together, we talk a couple of times a week. When we were at the WUSA Festival last week, they protected me like mother hens, encouraging me to take it easy and constantly asking, "What do you need me to do?"

Part of being on a team is paying close attention to those around you. Eventually, you learn to read even your most introverted teammates, and that helps with communication on and off the field. For instance, when I first met Kristine Lilly, she was a bit reserved, not the kind of person who puts herself out there. How was she feeling on any given day? In the beginning, I never knew. It took me quite a while to get to know her, on the inside. Now, it takes just a glance to check in. And when I see my other teammates coming into the locker room first thing in the morning, I can tell if they slept well, and what kind of attitude they're likely to have on the practice field.

Still, it's easy to go through the motions, and not truly get to know someone. I ask Cameron all the time about his teammates, even what they wore—not because the details are important, but because I'm trying to make sure he's aware of the people in his surroundings. Being attentive to others, listening to them, is a way to connect with your teammates and to build your relationships.

There are many small but significant ways you can further this connection. I try to remember to show my teammates I'm thinking about them and to make them feel good. Aly Wagner likes to chew gum, so I'll bring a pack and put it in her locker. Abby Wambach likes music, so I'll put a disk of her favorite tunes in the CD player in the locker room and call out, "Abby, this song goes out to you!" I bought a sewing machine and made my teammates cloth belts. Recently, I surprised my roommates with tickets to a Madonna concert.

Some of these are obviously silly little things. They don't all take a huge effort, but I think they can lighten the load, and make both your teammates and you feel good about being together.

The main aspect of being a part of a team is respecting one another. You work with other people on the field and in school, and, in one way or another, you will work with others for the rest of your life. Whatever the position of a teammate, respect the fact that she has earned it. Her voice is as important as everyone else's. Her opinion matters. On our team, enormous respect goes to someone like Tiffany Roberts. She's been on and off the National Team since 1995, but not one day in training goes by when she isn't working intensely. She may not make the traveling roster to Japan or Canada, but that doesn't deter her from working hard. Everyone talks about her: "Look at TR [her nickname]; it's so impressive." And we tell her so when we meet up after training in the locker room.

Even on a team as tight as ours, sometimes it's necessary to speak up in order to be heard. When a coach puts out a drill and asks, "Does everyone understand?" I'm not afraid to ask questions. (I think my teammates would like me to shut up sometimes!) The team experience gives me the confidence to speak up and get clarity on something I don't understand. I've built mutual respect with my teammates. They know I've dedicated myself to my efforts. Team sports is about opening yourself up to others, and knowing that although a 100 percent success rate is very unlikely all the time, you have to be very courageous to take risks and be evaluated on a daily basis.

I go out onto the field every day and I'm analyzed, critiqued by everyone—fans, coaches, the media, and the teams we play against. But I will always have the support and respect of my teammates.

In earlier chapters, I talked about extending your hand to other players, both teammates and opponents. I meant it literally and figuratively. It's easy to extend a gesture to another player, even to your rivals, but do you mean it? Currently, I'm fighting with other players (Kylie Bivens, Cat Reddick, Heather Mitts, Danielle Slaton, Joy Fawcett, Kate Markgraf) for the same position on my team. That doesn't mean I'm not going to share information with them, and give them the benefit of my experience. I would be doing them, the team, and myself a disservice if I didn't.

As you can see, a team is a weave of people—their personalities, abilities, and emotions. That's the beauty of the game, and of life.

chapter eight: perspiration plus inspiration . . .

Like anything else we're drawn to, you'll know you're inspired by the game when you can't stop figuring out ways to spend more time playing. You think about it all the time; whenever you're awake, you want to be around it. If you're like me and soccer is your game, you may find yourself dribbling a ball around the house, nutmegging chairs, playing 1 v 1 with the dog, and driving your mom to distraction kicking the ball against the garage door at all hours. Finding inspiration is like falling in love—or at least like making a really good friend. You hang out all day, yet as soon as you part, you feel as if something is missing. At least with a friend, you can always call her up—it's harder to keep dribbling when a parent tells you to knock it off.

My mother once gave me this quote from Henry David Thoreau: "Go confidently in the direction of your dreams. Live the life you've imagined." This was always her mantra: If you're going to do it, do it with confidence, and live how you believe you should. After my mom passed away, I taped that quote in a prominent place in my kitchen. It's a daily reminder of her, and of why I get up in the morning.

Whether it be sports, music, or some other hobby, if you're lucky, you'll eventually find that activity you love, the one that grabs your imagination and inspires you to play and practice it all the time. Before I found soccer, I took ballet. While tutus, balance bars, and point shoes may be a dream for some girls, they didn't make a dancer out of me. (However, I do believe it helped my rhythm and balance.) My neighbor Dori Whipple remembers me at a dance recital, defiantly stamping my feet and rolling my eyes. Needless to say, I didn't wear my hair in a bun for long.

When it came to soccer, though, it was love at first kick. Up to that point, I had never worn a uniform. In my limited experience, only boys got to wear them, so it was like forbidden fruit when I got one of my own. At Halloween, all the other girls wore princess or dance costumes; I donned shin guards and my new shorts and jersey. I wore my uniform to bed. For me, the uniform was so connected to the game that I hated to take it off. I had no idea if I was any good, but I always wanted to play, and just the ritual of donning my uniform was enough to get me excited. I never had time for tutus, but I've loved wearing a uniform ever since we picked up my first one at the store.

But it was much more than the gear that got me hooked on the game. Most of the other girls played inside with dolls, but I loved being outside. I was one of those kids who wouldn't come into the house until my mother yelled that it was time for dinner. I was an active kid (some might say "overactive") so the nonstop action of soccer was a good match for me. Becoming a soccer player wasn't a conscious choice. Like many kids, I didn't find the game I loved; it found me. One day my parents and I walked hand in hand down the street, and they signed me up to play in the league that they heard was starting in my neighborhood. It was as simple as that.

READY, SET . . . PLAY

Ever since I discovered athletics at age six, the adrenaline jolt of being called in for a game has never failed to give me a charge. At the Algarve Cup in the spring of 2004, when the coaches called my name to go in for the second half of a game, it was like being summoned for the very first time. I was *so* excited, I couldn't contain my adrenaline. I got all revved up over a game I've played a thousand times, just like I used to when I was a little kid. Being on the field was fantastic.

Like an artist seeing the possibilities of a blank canvas, I'm inspired by the field of play and all the subtleties that transpire on the pitch. I love how players can manipulate the ball in ways that seem to go against the laws of physics—to put a spin on the ball and make it come back, to effortlessly loft it forty yards downfield, to be able to lift it over someone's head or strike a full volley without breaking stride. The artistry of someone like the English star Kelly Smith, whom I watched at a recent WUSA Festival and who played against me with the Philadelphia Charge, fills me with awe. She got a ball on the left-hand side of the field and casually invited the defensive pressure. Then, she dipped her right shoulder, faking as if to go forward, and cut the ball with the outside of her left foot. The defenders took the bait. In two touches Smith was past the overcommitted defenders, and in another instant she was clear on the backside of them and going to goal. That's inspiration!

SPARKING THE FIRE

My friend Philippe Blin, a coach with the Pleasanton Valley Soccer Club, whose Under 19 girls' team won the National Championships in 2004, knows that while he cannot force his girls to love soccer, he can help to inspire them. Ever young at heart, Philippe likes to take on the role of announcer during team practice. "Today, you are the National Brazilian Team, here to help the great Pelé win the World Cup," he'll declare, getting the girls motivated. The thing that always impresses me about this approach is that while invoking soccer greats, Philippe never forgets that, above all, the game needs to be fun for kids.

That's something that parents of budding athletes should also remember. First and foremost, sports are games—and learning any game should be fun. If they can keep that in mind, and leave it to their children to discover their own love for sport (or art, literature, science, or what have you), it'll add not just to their enjoyment but to their willingness to work hard, focus, concentrate, and very likely improve over time. As Philippe and other coaches understand, the only way to bring out kids' greatness is to let them find their own inspiration.

No matter the level of competition, the fun factor cannot be overrated. Research backs this up. Every study I have seen shows that the single strongest motivating factor by far for children's participation in sports is having fun. And every one of those studies lists constant parental pressure and an exclusive emphasis on winning as the biggest reason for losing interest or dropping out. In other words, success should be measured primarily in units of fun, and not according to the win-loss tally; young players cite team spirit, a sense of belonging, and skills development among their top reasons for involvement in almost any activity.

When I give a talk, I make sure to tell this to young children, and to their parents. A coach can give them information; parents can give them advice and try to motivate them; teachers can help with homework; but only the individual, in the end, can light the fire. "I am here to tell you that you are awesome, if you want to be. Only you can make that choice," I say. And when these children master a skill they thought was beyond them, I love to see their eyes light up. "You did it!" I cheer for them. I think that simple message of empowerment allows them to find something in themselves they probably couldn't even name. In addition to having fun, that sense of self-discovery inspires them.

As a player, I knew from an early age I had something to contribute, but it was only with time that my own self-discovery prompted me to realize that I could also be a leader off the field. The first time I knew I had something to share was as a counselor at the San Jose Earthquakes soccer camp. There I was, a sixteen-year-old in charge of dragging eight-year-olds out of bed to get them to the field by seven A.M. It was no easy task. I was assigned to lead the warm-up. I remember that when dribbling around, the more enthusiastic I became, the more excited the campers were. The more I let them kick the ball away from me, to experience an opportunity to be successful, the more they got into it.

Inspiration is fostered when parents appreciate how their children really enjoy an activity, and find ways to support it. Children know when they are into something they're good at. They sense they have some talent, and they decide to pursue it.

I wish I could personally say to every young player out there, "Don't be too serious. Don't let things weigh you down. Don't let parental or peer pressure make you do something you ordinarily wouldn't want to do." But I'm a realist. Pressure and conflict wear away motivation. Girls more than boys face dilemmas that make them want to drop out of sports. But I wonder why children today, for example, are asked to choose between specializing in one sport and enjoying many. They will have to make choices, but I don't think it's healthy to force them to make certain ones too early. How do we keep the path clear for them so conflict doesn't interfere?

When my young player pen pal Teresa Rancadore's mother, Sandy, talks about her daughter playing in goal, it's with passion, but her mom keeps it simple. There's the excitement of her team playing up an age group, or of her going to a tryout—whether she'll make it or not—and the anticipation of going into junior high school. Sandy can take advantage of that excitement, yet she knows how to keep it from going over the edge. I admire the fact that she occasionally makes Teresa take a two-week break from the game, even though the time off drives her daughter crazy.

TENDING THE FLAME

If we lose that inner spark, even the support of our families and friends ultimately makes no difference—there's nobody but the individual herself who can rekindle that inspirational fire if it goes out.

After the 1999 World Cup, my teammate Briana Scurry grew estranged from soccer. She lost her interest in the game and, as a result, was not the starting goalkeeper in the 2000 Olympics. We had plenty of faith in Siri Mullinix, our new starting keeper, but the players wanted Briana to get back to being herself. She wasn't the Bri we had known; there was a level of intensity lacking, and an element of joy, it seemed to me. At practice, it was obvious her physical and mental focus had changed—and there was nothing the team could do about it.

We all go through those personal times, when events or other factors affect the way we function. After quite a while—and in her own time—Bri decided to return to soccer. We were happy she had found her way back, and having been left alone to make her own decision, she was able to create a genuine renewed commitment. This development boded well for her and our upcoming games. "Thanks so much for believing in me; it really means a lot," she communicated to the team. And she became a better goalkeeper by far than she had ever been, because she wanted it. Time, perspective, and being out of the mix is what got Bri back into the game, and she has been the starting keeper ever since. In my experience, kids need even more understanding than we veteran pros.

If we want to help young people discover their own inspiration and motivation, we have to realize just how many ways you can define success. Parents in particular can articulate what success is by understanding how it can extend beyond the context of the game. Coaches and families can make that success possible by making its other meanings tangible. A small move correctly executed can be enough to generate self-assurance, and that can spark all sorts of motivation. When I'm going through a tough time and need to feel reinspired to get my confidence back, Jerry gives advice that has worked for me. "Always go back to the simple things," he says. "Attempt a five-yard pass. Complete it successfully. Build from there." I use this technique all the time to unravel the complications and regain self-confidence.

At one point, when I played for the CyberRays, I got into a bit of a performance slump. Coach Ian Sawyers was trying to help me figure out the problem. He said, "You're one of the best players in the world right now, but you're not playing like it. You're not playing like yourself, not taking people on or being aggressive. Stop thinking and just play." When you try to do too much, my coach was telling me, you can get in your own way. I felt a heavy burden as the captain of the CyberRays and a National Team player, and thought that by analyzing every detail of my own play I could improve the situation. I was trying to take on the responsibility of being both a defender and an attacker—in order to win the game. So when that didn't happen, I got down on myself, and then nothing worked. When I went back to the simple things, the rest of my game took care of itself.

Even small successes inspire me, like winning a 50/50 ball, or clearing out a corner kick. Positive reinforcement inspires me. I soak up the comments people make. "When you and Aly Wagner came into the game at half time, you really changed things for the better. I appreciate your hard work, even though you only played a half," wrote a fan after a pre–2004 Olympics USA versus Japan match in Louisville. I remember how disappointed I was to miss the first half of that game, but with these kind words I gained the perspective to recognize that even small contributions to a win are important to celebrate.

REKINDLING THE FIRE WITHIN, by Briana Scurry

When we went into PKs in the 1999 World Cup final, I had a lot of confidence in our team to make their shots. So I knew I just needed to make one save, and we'd be fine. I didn't guess right on the first one, but I almost got the second. Then came the third. The last time I had looked at a shooter was in traveling soccer at age fifteen, but not since. For some reason (maybe it was divine intervention), I looked at this particular one, number 13. "This is the one," I said to myself, as she was walking toward the ball. Her body language was speaking as loudly as the crowd, and I knew in my gut I was going to save her shot.

Athletes have these great moments in sports, where they feel completely light, watching themselves as if they were standing outside of their bodies. I don't remember the save exactly. She took the shot, and I went to my left. The next thing I remember was the feeling that came over me when the whole thing was over.

Obviously, it was one of most dramatic conclusions to any sporting event ever. No one expected ninety thousand people in the stadium and forty million television viewers. That's one out of every six people in the country watching! Insane. That save made pictures that went all over the country, and all over the world.

What happened next is that literally overnight we became sensations. I went from being a complete unknown to being recognized on the street in every city where I went. It began right after the game, when celebrities had called the locker room, and now other people from everywhere were calling to say, "You guys are America's sweethearts." Fifty-year-old men would come up to me on the street and tell me they were crying after we won. We traveled from Oregon to Florida, and hopped from Leno, to Regis and Kathie Lee, to Rosie

O'Donnell. (I thought originally I'd go home and rest for a week after the World Cup, and get back to my life.) I was in New York seven times in three months.

Fortunately and unfortunately, my life flipped upside down. In the meantime, my metabolism was slowing down; I wasn't going to the gym as regularly as I had been, and I was eating random food at completely random times. In the next seven months, I gained thirty pounds.

A lot of people get out of shape in the off-season, but the weight gain was gradual enough for me not to notice how much I had put on, until I got on the scale in February at a hotel in Las Vegas at the ESPY awards (we won our category for best sports team of the decade), and I mumbled, "Oh, boy." I was mortified. (I thought my pants had been getting a bit tight. . . .)

My weight perpetuated some injuries. First, I pulled a quad muscle; then I got shin splints that turned into stress fractures. I can't say I really burned out. I was tired, though, from the whirlwind, and when I started playing again in February, with all the extra weight, my body wasn't doing what it normally did. We had a new coaching staff, and there was a lot more fitness required from the goalkeepers.

I had to leave the team for a few months because of my stress fracture. Siri Mullinix did well during my absence, and I lost my spot to her on the 2000 Olympics team. I was furious. I felt as if I was owed something. I blamed everyone but myself. I didn't feel as if I had had a fair shot, but in retrospect, it took me two years to realize that I was the one to blame. I got into shape, and down to my playing weight of 155, but I knew that my job was gone and that I would have to sit.

It was the night we lost in the Olympics and seeing pictures of myself overweight during those months that turned me around. I realized I didn't want to be bitter and angry. I didn't want to be on the top of the mountain in '99 and then just fall off. I didn't want to go out like that. My parents didn't raise me to be that kind of person. I wanted to reach my potential, and be the best Briana Scurry, goalkeeper for the United States.

I started running, doing cardio, and lifting weights. I hibernated in the gym. In the two winters between WUSA seasons, I spent six days a week there. I watched what I ate—no more Cheetos. I read books and went online, researching everything I could find to be the absolute fittest and healthiest.

When I think back on what had hurt me the most during that time, it was watching my team lose to Norway in the Olympics final and seeing them cry. I blame myself for not taking care of them. I feel that way to this day, and that's why I'm the way I am now—absolutely on top of my game. It's not only for myself, but also for them.

There aren't a lot of people who can say about what they do, "I'm the best in the world." But it comes with a lot of responsibility. I have seventeen other women who count on me, and I count on myself. My message is: Don't ever forget where you came from, and why you're doing what you do. And reach your highest potential.

Who do you want to be? What kind of mark do you want to leave on the world? That's what's important to me. My dad passed away a month ago, on Father's Day, and I want to continue his legacy. He was proud of me. Right now, I'm fired up. I want to be on the podium again, hearing the National Anthem.

LITTLE SPARKS OF INSPIRATION

I'm not superstitious, but there are rituals that I believe help us to create focus and reenergize ourselves. I have no set routine. I stick to just doing what I feel like at that time. If I'm watching a movie I don't get a chance to finish, I bring my portable DVD player on the team bus. Or I finish reading a book I'm in the middle of. I'll even dance or sing songs in the locker room if I'm in a playful mood. These are some of the ways I relax.

Others have their own techniques. Away from her busy household with three children, my teammate Joy Fawcett takes advantage of the pregame quiet to read constantly. Aly Wagner sports a lucky wristband, as does Cameron, who also listens to the song "Eye of the Tiger." Everyone has her rituals, from listening to special music, to polishing her cleats, to eating a special meal—in short, whatever helps get her into the moment.

Looking at the bigger picture can also help to inspire us. Casey, the cancer survivor who gave me a lock of his hair, has a special place in my life. I keep that lock of hair in my cleat bag. It helps me remember to live each day to its fullest. On that bag is also a carabineer, a connector used in rock climbing. It's from an exercise we did before the 1996 Olympics with Colleen Hacker, the National Team sports psychologist. We each held on to a carabineer, and then held on to each other in a circle, leaning one way, and then another. We were bound together by the carabineers, held up by the trust that we would never break our bond. I look at the carabineer before games to remember that our team is actually a chain, and we've all got to be strong.

For inspiration, I also keep a journal of my experiences. Currently, I've been looking back on my entries from the 1996 Olympics. It's a good way to remember positive scenarios. I record and watch great soccer games. When I'm a little down, I listen to music or I take out my first tournament T-shirt, which helps me remember why I started playing the game. I think back on all that practice I did in the front yard to enter that tournament's juggling competition, where I came in seventh out of about a hundred kids. Not bad, I tell myself. It's still a great memory, and it helps me focus not so much on the wins and losses but rather on the good times instead of the bad.

Some people put a lot of stock in players' numbers. I didn't choose number 6, my current playing number. It was the only number available when I originally made the National Team. When I got back onto the team in 1995 after a two-year absence, Debbie Keller, the player who was using number 6, gave it back to me. I thought that was a nice gesture. Now, Cameron wears number 6 as well. Some players feel very connected to their number, as if it's a part of their identity. In the days before names were put on the jerseys, numbers represented positions—with the lower numbers being defenders, number 9 being goal scorers, and number 10 being the playmakers. While I believe that the play (not the number) defines a player, I would never deny anyone her jersey mojo.

Of course, there are still other things that can inspire us. In the locker room of the Carolina Courage of the WUSA, there was a board with detailed statistics outlining each game—the win/loss, percentage of 50/50 balls, shots on goal, percentage of first balls won, etc. They kept track of it all so they could push themselves to work on what they needed to, and to celebrate what they did well.

THOSE WHO INSPIRE US

When I started playing soccer, I had no role models to inspire me on the field. No one in my neighborhood, or in my family, played the game. But the very first time I saw the professional team that would become my guiding light, the San Jose Earthquakes, I found my role model. He was George Best, and in my mind the name fit.

Before coming to San Jose in 1980, Best, a native of Belfast, Ireland, was a star forward for his country, and for Manchester United, scoring 137 goals for that team. Pelé, who knows something about greatness, once called Best "the greatest player in the world." I can still remember how he effortlessly dribbled around everyone in the penalty box and slipped the ball past the goalkeeper. It didn't look as if he even broke a sweat. He was the image of what I wanted to do when I was on the field. As soon as I saw him, I knew what I wanted to be.

Players like George Best gave me what we on the National Team are trying to give young children today—somebody to look to who has the same passion, dedication, dreams, and flair for the game.

This sort of inspiration, when you help ignite it in someone else, is not just contagious, it's reciprocal. For instance, as part of Nike's marketing plan for the 1999 Women's World Cup, some of the players' jerseys were marketed to young fans. It reminded me of when I was a small child at soccer camp, when counselors gave out Pelé, Franz Beckenbauer, and, yes, George Best jerseys to the kids to wear for the day if they did something special. The lucky young players would be presented with the shirt in front of all the campers. There was nothing I wanted more than to wear one of those jerseys, to feel as if I had accomplished something. So after that 1999 marketing campaign, the first time I saw someone wearing

"Chastain #6" it was unreal. Today, when I see those kids wearing my jersey, I feel that perhaps I've touched them in the same way I was touched all those years ago.

I get some amazing letters. Kids write about their dreams. I also get a lot of letters like the one from a parent who shared with her daughter a first-time experience at a women's professional soccer game. She wrote about how they could be together, and for those several hours, she could look at the amazement on her daughter's face. "I never knew we could share that kind of bond," she wrote. In addition to receiving letters and requests for autographed pictures, I sometimes get more interesting requests. I once autographed a Jogbra a boy was wearing at a game. I was impressed that he paid attention to women's soccer, and even more impressed that he was confident and courageous enough to wear that piece of women's clothing in public. Maybe it *is* about the bra!

These situations, and many others, motivate me to work harder, and dig deeper. It's inspiring to be in any situation that teaches you there's a level you haven't yet achieved. No matter how hard you work, or what you do, there's always more.

INSPIRING OUR CHILDREN by Gloria Averbuch

Studies show that the number one factor in influencing children to become involved in sports is parent role models. Brandi inspires her stepson Cameron by playing soccer with him, and, of course, his father's a coach. But we can't all play the game like Brandi Chastain, and we all can't coach like a pro. So we have to look for other ways to help guide our children.

Sometimes, the best we can do as parents is to realize when it's time for us to step back and let someone else fulfill an important role. So, find great coaches and players for your children to emulate. And don't be afraid to actively engage these people in your quest to connect them to your family. One of the reasons Brandi believes the National Team is so valuable to youth soccer is that, compared to most professional athletes, the players are very accessible. They mingle with the crowd after the game, taking time to sign autographs, and they even answer mail.

When my two soccer-playing teenage daughters (ages seventeen and fourteen) were very young, we used to invite the former English pros who coach in the area to dinner to talk soccer, or we took them out for a meal in exchange for kick-arounds with our girls. We also went to watch them play, and scouted out other high-level teams to watch. But it always boiled down to celebrating the girls' accomplishments, and helping them develop skills.

We kept track of fun games and challenges, like setting personal ball-juggling records, with lists we hung up in full view. The girls carried balls everywhere—even dribbling or juggling up to the school-bus stop every morning. We still keep a permanent training bag with balls and cones in the trunk of the car. It's amazing how many opportunities there are to use it. But we found other ways to naturally integrate the game into our lives, including investing in satellite TV, which is constantly tuned to soccer. Although my husband and I aren't soccer players, we still accompany the girls to the park when they play on their own, to serve and retrieve balls, and to express our respect and enjoyment of their dedication.

These independent efforts may just have been the most important factor in our children developing a true love of the game. Because we still make family outings out of independent training, our daughters grew up to be each other's favorite soccer partner. All these years later, if there is no organized soccer scheduled, they still insist on going out to play on their own. At the same time, soccer has given our family the opportunity to create an extraordinary bond. There has been many a small but unforgettable moment, as the sun sets and we've been out for hours, when we have shared a laugh, or talked about life, while the girls slam a ball against a concrete wall.

To this day, when they go off to soccer camps or tryouts, I uphold a tradition. I tuck humorous or inspirational notes into their bags, or stuff gum or chocolate bars inside their cleats. I frame their soccer photos and buy them soccer books. I continually share my pride in them, or express my thoughts on life and their game, by e-mailing them. It's become a ritual that those "mother's musings" are best absorbed via the written word.

In the end, we bring inspirational qualities to our children's sports other than simply the possibility to play with them. As Cameron points out, he learns a lot just by watching the way Brandi lives her life. If you are committed to your own work, and share with your children a passion and love for what you do, chances are they will bring that same love to their game. After all, that's what happened with Brandi and her parents.

ASPIRE TO INSPIRE

How do you reach out to your teammates? One youth player I know spent all weekend tie-dying T-shirts in her team colors, and putting them on the door handles of the each player's hotel room with a special note the night before a big game. I hear the Under 19 National Team recently got together before a big match to watch the movie *Miracle*, the story of the 1980 U.S. Olympics ice hockey team, before the championship game. What inspires you? Whatever it is, why not share it with your team. It's a great way to get them psyched, and also to exercise your leadership skills.

chapter nine: leadership material

Generally, no one becomes a leader overnight. But in a sense, I did, in two hard nights of soul searching. At least, I learned to recognize some important qualities of leadership that I had never paid much attention to be-fore. When Jerry banished me from practice at Santa Clara, I spent my two-day exile realizing that although I had the talent to be a good player, something was still missing from my game. Then it came to me: If I wanted to be a leader, I had to back that up with my play. In addition to game-day communication and performance, I needed to bring a commitment and enthusiasm for fitness I had not exhibited before. My ability to influence the people around me would be based not solely on my words or intentions, but on my actions and attitude as well. One of the major things I recognized about leadership then is that sometimes it's not so much who you are or what you say—it's what you do and how you do it.

These days, young players tend to be a lot more mature, and more serious about their sport, than they were in my day. Pressure makes diamonds, they say, and youth leagues are full of near gems. I think positive peer pressure from teammates can make a significant difference in a player's development. It can be difficult to motivate yourself when you're on your own. But if others around you are diligent, they can set the tone for you to follow. Today, players learn early that when they work hard, they tend to feed off one another. That was certainly true for me at Santa Clara. I needed to be among those hardworking people and be one of them as well.

When it comes to setting the tone for the team, though, the coach ultimately has the responsibility for creating an environment that both fosters and rewards leadership in players. As Jerry did with me, the coach must sometimes ask players who consistently detract from that environment to leave. Although I certainly wasn't a leader when I stormed off the Santa Clara fields, I returned with the intention to become one. Eventually, I was named captain of the team—and went on to captain my WUSA professional team as well. But I never would have gotten to that point without the coaches pointing out the direction.

Over the years, I've learned that leaders not only make decisions, but they have to live with the outcome. Whether it's the coach or captain, they step up and take control of the game. It's an important role that entails risk, responsibility, commitment, and accountability. Of course, where there are leaders, there must be followers, so perhaps it's assumed that not everyone needs to step into a leadership role. But that's not exactly the case. There are times on the field, and in life, no doubt, when every one of us will be called upon to be a leader. Don't be afraid of that calling. You will gain confidence by accepting that role when it is thrust upon you.

On the other hand, while you may be the captain, or considered the leader of the team, it's not always right to take charge at every moment. There are times you have to take a step back to listen, and become a follower. Those roles are constantly interchangeable. For example, I'm one of two central defenders with Joy Fawcett. At any given moment, depending on who has the better perspective, one of us will be calling out directions to the other and assuming the mantle of leadership on the back line. Joy is a co-captain of the team, but to her credit, she's never balked at being a follower when the situation calls for it. In games, the transition from leader to follower for us has become seamless. It's an important lesson in give and take.

Leadership is a vital part of the game, but it's not simple. Just like maneuvering the ball, there's an art and a skill to it. Each player sees the game, and processes information, differently. Sometimes you need to hold the ball, sometimes pass it; sometimes you try for a goal yourself, sometimes it's best to make an outlet pass. Similarly, teammates have to make the decision to follow one another and to do it as a unit so there is not chaos on the field. At times, someone may question a direction and make the choice not to follow, if she feels that that direction is not right—but if done consistently, that's going to get her in trouble with the coach and captains before too long. And that's what a solid understanding of teamwork helps avoid. Joy and I have been playing soccer together, and communicating, for fifteen years. Our on-the-field strategizing is constant and fluid. We've learned how to make it work.

THE LEADER WITHIN

I've known many types of leaders since I first stepped on the field. There are leaders who grow into the role, and those who seem to be born to it. These are leaders who take the initiative, who seek out information. They rally people. They are usually the ones you see running for class president, raising money for good causes, or planning a party. They're the movers who get things going. But sometimes you've got to *learn* how to do these things. I know I did.

I certainly wasn't the type of child to take control of every situation I encountered. I think I was that way on the inside, but I needed to shed my self-consciousness and learn to be confident on the outside. Many kids, I think, suffer from a similar lack of confidence in their leadership abilities, and they tend to test their skills only in moments when they feel safe. I see it in Cameron, for example. He puts a toe into the water, testing leadership among his teammates with his humor or work ethic. But it's only after he has seen that they are willing to follow that he dives in and takes charge.

Julie Foudy, on the other hand, is one of those natural leaders. She exemplifies the qualities leaders need: the ability to communicate, an ease in fitting in with different groups of people, and an intelligence coupled with a great sense of humor. She wears her leadership comfortably. As a co-captain with experience since 1995, she fluidly juggles the personal styles, desires, and problems of the team with those of the coaching staff.

One time, we had a 3 v 3 tournament, and Julie's team didn't win a single game. But there wasn't one of those games in which she didn't attempt to work harder to show her team they could do it; or, using her voice, she constantly communicated and encouraged her teammates. Even though inside she may have been burning in frustration, she never let up and never let it show. Is the fact that the team didn't win a failure of Julie's leadership? I don't think so. It would be a failure, though, if she gave up pushing and encouraging them.

There isn't necessarily one type of captain who's best to lead the National Team, a 3 v 3 team, or any team. There are many successful models. Most people think that leaders have to be people you can recognize as soon as they enter a room. Julie is definitely that kind of person. But Joy Fawcett, another National Team leader, doesn't fit the stereotypical mold, and is nonetheless an effective leader. She works hard every day and goes about getting better. She is very soft-spoken, but she always finds a way to get the job done and to get people to respect and emulate her.

The National Team benefits from the leadership of both Julie and Joy. They bring different attributes and skills to the job of captaining the team. The result is a balanced leadership that can be very successful. It comes down to their personalities, reflected by their positions: Julie is at the center of our offense; Joy is the heart of our defense. Julie the attacker is outgoing, and Joy the protector is relatively shy. Julie is always looking at the big picture, and Joy is a focused problem solver. The rest of us players benefit by being surrounded by those who share different traits, and yet who can both guide and challenge us.

There's an important aspect of humility in leadership. Mia Hamm is a perfect example. She never takes credit for her success, but she'll be the first one to take responsibility if something doesn't go well. She's the one who will say: I could have done more; I could have made a better pass; I should have had more focus. Even so, Mia wants others to realize that it's about more than one person. Although questions are directed toward her at a press conference, she'll draw another player sitting with her into the interview. She always tells the media, "My goal wasn't because of one person. My teammates worked so hard."

Mia also shows leadership in her willingness to contribute in any way she can. Some days, it's not going well for her offensively. She'll shoot a ball ten yards over the goal or be stymied by defenders around the box, but she'll be busting her tail on defense, chasing players down, and slide tackling.

My first model leaders weren't even soccer players. They were my parents. My father led by example, taking over the team-coaching job even though he knew little about soccer, and he led other parents in getting involved in their children's sports. My mom encouraged everyone in my soccer environment, and she was recognized among her peers at work as a recipient of service awards. My parents' leadership styles differed from each other as well. My dad was more like Joy Fawcett, a quiet type who inspired others by his devotion and hard work. My mom was more vocal; in fact, she was very outspoken. (I guess the apple doesn't fall far from the tree!)

LEAD ON! by Julie Foudy

The qualities of a good leader are the same both on and off the field. You have to be a good observer and a good communicator. You really have to be able to take the pulse of your team, to be the link between the coaches and the players, and to negotiate a lot of feedback. The captains have always had a good give-and-take with all the coaches who have come onto the National Team. The captains and the coaching staff work very hard together to make sure the team gels. So I think, as a captain, you really have to understand the team, and communicate that understanding to the coaches.

I've always been a captain. I was a captain of my high school, club, and college soccer teams. I think the leadership instinct is innate. You're drawn to it. I've always been the one to speak up. I'm fairly opinionated. I've always been extremely competitive and disciplined and have wanted to do well, and not just in sports.

On the National Team, I learned by watching the other captains, such as Carla Overbeck. I was co-captain with her, and she is one of the best leaders I've ever seen. Her tone on the field, and her attitude off, were remarkable. She was always firing up the team, or calming them down when necessary. The two of us had a balance. Carla would get upset and go off on something, and I'd start laughing. Or I'd lose it, scream at the referee, and I'd catch her cracking up at me. There we were, laughing in the middle of the game. She had a wonderful way about her. Off the field she was a great listener and communicator as well.

I have an incredibly intense side that comes out on the field. I can be the first one to light a fire under someone if things aren't going well. At the same time, I'm a big believer in keeping things light. When we're having fun, and thinking less, and just playing and feeling it—then we're really good. In a big tournament, like before the World Cup, we're often dancing and laughing and messing around in the locker room. There are some people who have their Walkmans on, like Bri, and for her that says to me that she's completely focused and not distracted. Then I just know she's going to have a great game. But for me as a player, and for the team, I think the lighter side has always helped. It counters those high-pressure moments of the World Cup and the Olympics. People always ask us, "Isn't there tremendous pressure?" "No," I answer. "It's an opportunity to show the world how good we are."

True, I can get carried away with that lighter-side attitude. There are times I'll make a sarcastic remark when humor is probably not the best idea. The other day Mia said to me, "Can you just be serious for five seconds?" "Okay," I told her. I counted down, and could barely last that long.

One of the most trying times for us all is when an eighteen-person team is announced. Thirty or so players are fighting for a spot, and you've played with some of them for a long time who don't make it. On one hand, you want the team to be named, so the focus can be narrowed to the eighteen players, but you also recognize how difficult it is for the ones left off. Dealing with all of them is simply a responsibility the leader takes on.

This time around, Christie Welsh, who didn't make the 2004

Olympics roster but who I think is one of the future stars of the game, said to me after the list of names went up, "It's frustrating when your best isn't good enough." I try to get players like Christie to understand that they are the next generation, and are prime for the next Olympics.

Coming off the 2000 Olympics loss was very tough. We played probably the best final we have ever played. "How could we not have won that?" I continually asked myself. You can't tell your team, "That's okay." Because it's not okay we lost. The reason this team has been so good for so long is that we don't settle for "That's okay." Instead, I told them, "Let's remember this, and carry it with us always. What lessons can we extract from the experience?" I want us to be on the top step of the Olympics podium again.

After that final, our players were in the locker room crying, and at the same time, we could hear Norway next door singing "We Are the Champions." It was like when they did the centipede after beating us in the 1995 World Cup. The pain of that experience is imprinted and was a big motivator for us in 1999.

As the captain, you ask yourself all the time, "What could I have done?" Even now, going into the 2004 Olympics, I ask myself, "Have we covered all the bases; what, if anything, are we lacking?" because sometimes, the smallest things can make the biggest difference.

LEADERSHIP MATERIAL

Empathy, being sensitive and understanding of others, is one of the assets of a great leader. Without a read on others' emotions—their enthusiasm, motivation, inspiration, sadness, or joy—you'll never know where your team can go, and how to get them there, because you'll have no sense of the pulse of the people.

In turn, it's often hard for young players not to assume that a leader is somehow superior, and therefore set apart. If a leader understands that notion, she can try to include others. If a leader empowers her teammates, the group will not feel there is a separation and will recognize that everyone has a voice. I'm more than ten years older than some of my teammates, with much more experience, but I keep in mind at all times that they, too, have something to share. Ideas are traded freely. The veterans maintain an open atmosphere so that rookies and experienced players can mix easily. It must be surprising for some of the new players to walk into the locker room and have National Team veterans like Mia, Kristine, and Julie turn to them for input. But we remember starting out, and we know that newcomers bring more than their skills to the team. They have a fresh perspective to contribute, too.

Experience has certainly put me in a good position to empathize with those around me. I've been both a starter and a reserve. I've been injured, and I know that can feel alienating and lonely. On a recent trip with the National Team, I encouraged Angela Hucles and Danielle Slaton, two other injured players, to come with me to the gym. I kept up a steady stream of encouragement—we were pushing one another—while we rode bikes. We worked out harder as a unit than we would have individually. Being together served a dual purpose—to get fit and to stay connected to the team environment.

Perspective is another important aspect of leadership. That means seeing the bigger picture. At a high level of play, you have to have passionate commitment. Working hard is a given. However, if a group is constantly being pushed to its limit, players will exhaust themselves or burn out. A good leader monitors the energy level so that doesn't happen. It's great to be passionate and serious about what you do, but you should maintain a fundamental understanding that it's still only a game, and that you're aware of life's priorities. Good leaders know when to push and when to ease up. It's challenging refs when they make bad calls on your teammates, but backing down before that yellow card flashes. It's about making little suggestions to young players on their field position, and cautioning sideline parents when they're ruining the game for their kids. Ultimately, leadership comes when you're able to recognize the mood and the needs of the team, to know when to move ahead, or when to take a step back, when you have the courage to tell your teammates to work harder, or go to your coach and tell him or her what the team needs.

SPOKEN LIKE A LEADER

Soccer is a complicated game. It requires doing many tasks at once. The brain is pulled in different directions. That makes the soccer field a challenging environment, even for the best leaders, because communicating on the field is much more immediate than sitting down and having a conversation. In our game, there are no time-outs, and on-the-field communication has to be instant and precise. You can't lay things out point by point and take the time to explain every last detail. You have time for one or two words, maybe a sentence at most. And you often have to get them out during the run of play.

People have both physical and emotional responses to what they hear. Players, particularly young ones, need time to develop the skills that combine that thinking and reasoning process with their physical actions. A leader recognizes that and reacts calmly even if there's some confusion.

Still, it's important for each individual team to discover a language that makes sense to the members. But you've got to learn to speak up in the first place. Like anything you do repeatedly, the more you communicate, the more comfortable you will become. If you don't know what to say at game time, try speaking up in practice, where you can focus on overemphasizing what's important until it becomes natural. Jerry even does a drill in practice in which everyone has to talk. You can't receive or make a pass without calling out a direction. It helps everybody find her voice.

Cameron and I often discuss how best to reach people as it connects to our game. He and I play the same position, so we experience a lot of the same issues. In turn, I try to help him tailor his approach to communication, depending on the individual. "How do we get through to people?" I ask. What do we do if they don't listen, understand, or respond? "You can't speak to Cory the same way you do to Eric," I tell him, referring to his teammates. "They're different people. You have to find different ways to connect with each one."

I remind him that this is a great life lesson as well, because it's something you face in many areas besides on the soccer field. No matter what you do, you will encounter situations, (and people) that seem similar, but that require very different approaches. Field leaders can be very vocal without offending anyone. It's all about tone and making sure your message is constructive (do this) instead of destructive (don't do that).

Sometimes Cameron tells his team, "We have to work harder." I know he has a couple of players in mind, but he doesn't want to single them out. "Work harder" is too general, I tell him. I advise him to give specific information directed to specific people. In the game, players respond best to precise and personalized advice, like, "Shannon, drop back and left" or "Julie, force her outside."

For effective communication on the field, we have to use language we can all understand. The more specific you can be, the better you will be understood. Some words or phrases are fairly simple in soccer terms, and we know what they mean. When you call for a pass by saying "space" or "feet," the player generally knows how hard to pass the ball just hearing that word. But communication can get much more complicated during an unfolding soccer game. If you want to instruct a teammate, don't just yell "pressure," or "man on"; say "pressure right," or "man on your left [or behind]." (I say this to Jules a lot.) On the National Team, when the goalkeeper shouts "Out!" we all know that means get out of the penalty box. When she says "Keeper!" we know she's going for the ball, so we get in the path of an attacker, or behind the keeper to guard the goal.

Like on the National Team, Santa Clara solves any potential confusion with a unique system to help clarify communication. The team uses a vocabulary list of words and phrases, which all players must know. Critical communication is often necessary in a split second, so they all have to be armed with their vocabulary. For example, when a defender is too close, and it is dangerous to make a small pass, you say "too tight"; more words than that will take too long and the ball may be turned over, so a short phrase keeps communication clear and flowing.

Our National Team psychologist Colleen Hacker does many interactive team exercises in which different people have to lead or follow, and in different ways. Before the 2003 Women's World Cup, we did one in which, at times, one person was blindfolded, or could not speak and could give only hand signals. This helped us learn alternative means to enhance our communication on the field.

POSITIVE LEADERSHIP

Sometimes, what you need to give isn't instruction or critique, but simply well-timed, unconditional support. A good leader understands that.

We were playing Germany in the early rounds of the 1999 Women's World Cup. The atmosphere was already emotionally charged. It was a full stadium, and the crowd was so loud that despite the fact that there was no offensive pressure, I still couldn't hear Briana Scurry from only fifteen yards away. In the confusion, I scored an own goal (i.e., I put the ball into my team's net, giving the opposition a goal). For anyone who has ever had this experience, you know how devastating it can be. I sighed and put my head down. It was 1–0.

Carla Overbeck, our captain at the time, could have said to me, "What were you thinking?" or "That was awful"—any negative comment imaginable. Instead, she gave me perspective, helped me relax, and empowered me by reminding me that I had a purpose. She told me, "Come on, Brandi. We've got plenty of game left, and you're going to make a difference. You're going to be part of the reason we win." I pulled myself together and thought, She's right. We have a lot of time. I'm out here for a reason." At a critical moment, she used compassionate communication to get through a really tough time, and to turn a potentially negative situation into a positive one. Late in the game, the score was 2–1, Germany leading. We had a corner kick. I was the near-post runner, and the ball went over my head. It got knocked back across the goal, which I was facing. It was just about to go past me, but I slid and got it on a half volley. I scored a goal. It was a clean slate. I had scored one for them, and one for us. I knew everything was okay. We went on to win the game, 3–2.

In the locker room afterward, I thanked Carla for helping me through that moment. She is also a great leader because she never accepts any of the praise. "I didn't do anything. I knew you'd be fine," she replied.

Not every last word intended to lift someone up needs to be an encouraging one, however. Sometimes, in exercising a leadership role, I'm going to get on someone. I'm very passionate about what I do. For example, Thori Bryan was my teammate on the CyberRays. Because she had experience on the National Team, my expectations of her were high. I was on her case a lot. If she made a mistake, I'd encourage her, "Come on, you can do better than that."

There are people who have a hard time with this style of leadership, but if you see it as part of the game, you can benefit from it. With Thori, some days she accepted what I said, and some days she didn't receive my criticism so well. How something is accepted, or not, depends as much on how it's said as on the recipient's mood and personality. That's why it's also a good idea to balance commands with positive encouragement whenever possible. "Way to go," "Nice tackle," a pat on the back, a thumbs-up, or an arm around a teammate's shoulder at half time—these are all gestures that let your teammates know you support them.

Overall, I think Thori accepted how tough I was on her, because her standards for herself were high. But you've got to be very sensitive under such circumstances. We had plenty of conversations about it, and I explained to her that sometimes I get caught up, and that things perhaps come out sounding not exactly as I mean them. I apologized if I was too tough. In fact, I told the entire team, "You guys need to get on me, to hold me accountable." Teams have to find acceptable ways to help their leaders, because those leaders need feedback to do their jobs well. We grew to the point where we could have this kind of openness. I didn't have to be ultra-careful about what I said, but I tried to remember to keep it positive regardless.

LEARNED LEADERSHIP

We had a player on my youth team, the Horizon, who was not as good as the others, but she came to every practice and worked as hard as anyone else. I remember my dad, who was the coach, being very adamant about supporting her and giving her equal time and attention. The same was true for any new players. This made an impression. He was teaching me something. Perhaps that's why, years later, I make it a point to go out of my way to embrace the newcomers, and those on their way up. I'm proud of the fact that when Shannon Boxx was interviewed about first joining the National Team, she singled me out, saying how good it made her feel that I pulled her aside and told her, "You belong here." Just last month, I invited the entire Under 21 National Team over to our house for dinner. That's thirty-five people, but we made room for all of them, and I made them feel right at home by telling them they had to do the dishes afterward!

I think leadership and communication are probably the aspects least attended to, and at the same time the aspects most difficult to get a handle on. Coaches and parents need to realize this, because in the beginning, they are the de facto leaders. Young players are consistently asked to practice and emphasize skill and technique, but very few people spend time teaching them leadership. One player or another will stand out as willing to give it a try, so we let the chips fall where they may and those people figure out leadership on their own. On the college or National Team level, where winning and losing plays a greater role, however, consistent leadership is crucial. To get the most out of the game, and to prepare our youth players for the big leagues—and for life in general—I think youth teams should appoint multiple leaders, such as a "captain of the week." This should be made a revolving role so that all the players can be leaders, which affords everyone an opportunity to learn the necessary skills. As with any aspect of the game, or of life, there is no substitute for experience.

Also, for those involved in coaching, I'd recommend spending fifteen minutes or so in each team meeting discussing the value and qualities of a good team captain and of leadership. Over time, in regular meetings, the team could single out a different player and discuss the qualities he or she brings to that role. Keep it positive, and explore why that person would be a good leader. What are his or her traits and abilities? Recognizing every player individually helps each one to see his or her best qualities in the eyes of others, how each may carry out a leadership role, and it makes everyone recognize that each player is crucial to the group.

Just remember, while a good coach can help a young leader, it's not entirely the coach's responsibility to empower that player. It's also a personal journey on the athlete's part. A relationship between the coach and the players, including the captain, doesn't just happen. It develops over time, and with a certain talent of both parties. Learning when and what to say, and how to read people, is a process from which coaches, parents, and players can all benefit.

chapter ten: making the cut

Climbing the ladder in youth sports shouldn't seem ruthless and cutthroat. It shouldn't devastate a player's confidence, although it can feel that way to a young person. But being a standout athlete can have unintended consequences. One of the most difficult scenarios for a young soccer player to deal with is being inappropriately pushed to face older, tougher, and stronger opponents, which can spoil her enjoyment of the game—and in the worst cases lead to injury and psychological problems.

For instance, I know one talented girl who, at only ten years old, was forced to "play up." Her parents claimed the girls her own age just weren't good enough, so she was moved first to a team a year ahead, then two, and eventually even four. Finally, at age fourteen, she found herself on an Under 18 team, where she lasted only a year. During that time, she struggled with injury, and the physical and social frustration of being an eighth-grader playing with high school seniors. She ultimately quit, took a break from playing, and eventually found a team her own age. What was the point of bouncing from team to team? Was she really so good that she couldn't find a challenging enough environment? Or was she just a victim of her parents' well-intentioned but clearly misguided ambitions? The result was clear: Instead of growing horizontally—enriching and deepening her game on a manageable level—she was pushed vertically—up and up, to higher levels of play. I have seen many examples of this sort of crash-and-burn scenario, when parents and sometimes even the players themselves assume that the higher the level of play, the better.

The truth is, as often as not, the unconsidered pressure that comes with this pushing upward robs young players of some of the best aspects of the game. When I'm conducting a clinic, a player sometimes will catch my eye. I can tell she is a cut above the rest by the way she touches the ball, or by the way she receives it using various surfaces of her feet. I can see that she is well balanced both on and off the ball, meaning she's balanced whether she is part of the play or not. But physical gifts should not be mistaken for competitive or psychological maturity. Despite an abundance of talent, a player may remain immature for many reasons. Attitude and commitment are a big part of striving to reach loftier goals; but there's no guarantee that skills, often judged out of context with the rest of a young player's game, will mean that player is prepared for a higher level. And as we've seen, the dangers of mistaking mere ability for mentality and experience can have harmful consequences.

Understanding the whole player comes only with experience. A veteran coach or someone who has been around the game a lot can recognize issues players and their families often miss. So when considering your level (or that of your children), recognize that the level you choose is only part of the equation that determines your reaching your potential. You'll also need maturity, practice, experience, and hard work to catch the eye of a coach or scout for a more advanced team.

Remember, the player-development system, in theory, is designed to make the decision for you. As often as not, the appropriate level will actually select you. Tryouts, seasoned coaches, and evaluators will assess where you belong. But that's only part of the process. There are other questions that need to be asked, such as, What kind of competitive experience do you have? And, perhaps more important, What do you want from the game? Don't just assume the obvious—that you want the team where you can play and win, and at the highest possible level. Ask yourself, Are you ready for not just the physical demands of advancing to a higher level, but also the commitment, and the mental and social challenges as well?

There are all sorts of aspects to selecting a level of play. While you want to be stretched, you don't want to be in over your head. You hope to be challenged by coaches who create a model for new and increasingly difficult tasks. You want a healthy environment, promoting and developing the right physical, mental, and emotional aspects of the game. Socially, you want to get along, and although it may not be the number-one priority, it helps that your parents and family feel they fit in as well.

There are a couple of boys on Cameron's team who aren't as good overall as the other players. They sit on the sideline; sometimes, they don't play more than half the game. Although they each have qualities they bring to the team (one of them, for example, is very fast, and the others are inspired by that), and they really like the boys they're playing with, at some point, their ability to develop their skills will dictate whether or not they are able to remain on the team, or to win more playing time.

On the other hand, success doesn't always come with how many minutes you play. I think making a commitment and fulfilling it can also be a measure of success. Going to practice every day, winning six of the ten races in training, or achieving victories in small-sided games are all laudable accomplishments. Having the courage to be evaluated on a daily basis by the coach, the players, and even the spectators—that's also success. Having a good time with the team when they travel to play in a tournament can also be a triumph of sorts.

MAKING THE CUT

Soccer players, like many athletes, are judged by subjective measures. Different coaches, players, and parents see different qualities. Self-confidence gets you to the sign-up sheet at a particular tryout; making the team is up to the selectors. One may feel you meet the standard; another may want something more from you, or from the overall team, that you can't provide. Ultimately, coaches get to make choices with which you may or may not agree. Accepting this is part of the process.

At the same time, understanding the game, and yourself—your strengths and weaknesses—will give you insight into how you may fit into a given system or deemed fit to participate in a certain level of play. Sure, some players are simply better than others, but that's not all there is to team selection. For example, I've seen some players who aren't the most physically talented, but they make teams based on their understanding of the game.

I have been part of the selection process on the high school and collegiate level. There are the obvious things you look for, but there are many other layers. The majority of people who watch the game look only at the obvious, the part with the ball—someone who is kicking, running at it, defending, or trying to take it away. Generally, as an evaluator, I watch players in pairs or small groups. I try to determine if there's something exceptional about an individual, whether attacking or defending. I watch to see if a player gives up when she loses the ball. Then, I'll watch larger groups to see how individual players interact with others. I want to see if they have a tendency only to push forward. Or do they get back to defend? Of course, I'm looking for skill, but also for the psychological factors—such as whether a player is assertive, or instead tends to "hide" from the action.

Once you've been through the selection process enough times, you can pick out the traits that will likely endure. Maturity, for example, manifests itself early in the greater players. I had a chance to see National Team players Danielle Slaton and Aly Wagner when they were about eleven years old. Even then, Danielle had physical talent; she was stronger and faster than the majority of others. But she also had mental toughness and a quick mind. When new concepts were introduced, she was the first player to ask questions and to make sure things were clear so she could implement them right away. And in soccer summer camp, I remember not only Aly's exceptional touches and movement on the ball but also her remarkable self-assurance on the field.

Of course, there's talent and potential, and then there's the so-called politics of the environment. Whatever level you aspire to, you will get the most out of your sports experience if you decide that it is always best to take the high road. No matter what happens in tryouts, continue to work hard. And if you're not initially successful, try again; even if you don't reach your ideal, maybe you'll discover there is a better place, and a better opportunity, elsewhere. Don't forget, the process is endless—just look at any top team in the nation, and you'll find men and women who never even played high school ball. Trust me, there will always be other tryouts and other opportunities in which to prove yourself.

It's always a risk to put yourself out there, but I believe it's a worthwhile risk. I've done it my entire career, and I've learned that even if I'm not up to the challenge at the moment, I can take some satisfaction that I went for it. On the other hand, remember that coaches often have only a small window of time, over one or maybe two days, to see everyone. In that limited time, sometimes a player can't show everything, or a coach can't see everything. I always tell players that at the next possible opportunity, they should absolutely go back and try again.

AIM, AGE, AND ABILITY— THREE FACTORS FOR FINDING YOUR LEVEL

Aim:

Personally, I advocate playing in the most challenging setting in which you feel comfortable. In other words, I think it's best to find an environment in which you can thrive, but that also challenges you so you have some room to develop. And remember, challenges can be incremental. If they seem insurmountable, you're probably in the wrong place. Find the right level to start, and it will always be easier to work your way up.

Age:

It doesn't matter what you call your league—pee wee, recreational, travel, or premier—the focus for very young players should be on skill development, not necessarily on winning. Obviously, the younger the child, the more basic the game should be— to the point of not even keeping score in the case of very small children. There will be plenty of time to move up, but skipping the early lessons of development can not only deprive a player of focus on the basics, but also fail to nurture her simple joy of the game. By avoiding the pressure to get results, the pure exhilaration of running around, having fun, and making new friends becomes emphasized, which in turn can lead to greater gains down the road. I know how vitally important this is from experience, since, fortunately, most of my early years were spent playing the game in low-pressure environments.

Ability:

Ultimately, in most cases, basic ability will determine your level of play. There is what is called the four pillars of soccer: tactical, technical, physical, and psychological. They are the basis of the game, and of player evaluation. To narrow in on those, I list the following subcategories to help examine a player: composure, focus, passion, and work ethic.

SETTING THE BAR

How do you know you're on the right level? While a tough environment on a higher level might include an honest analysis or harsh critique, a player shouldn't feel lost or left behind in any way. A challenging environment is good, but you need some measure of success or sign of possible future advancement. If you're pushed to the point where you feel you can't possibly do more, but then you come through, that's positive. Likewise, when you go away from practice, intent on figuring it out, on coming up with solutions—that's a good sign. When my youth team Horizon dissolved, and I moved on to the Under 16 West Valley Cougars, I was with new people in a new environment, and I was out of my comfort zone. But I was also learning, developing, and having a blast. The same thing happened the first time I went to Europe to play, and the first time I went to National Team training. All of these experiences gave me a taste of the levels on which I knew I could, and wanted to, play, and of the amazing challenges those levels offered.

On the other hand, sports is no fun if you're getting "beat up" all the time. If your self-confidence is perpetually low, or if you feel that no matter what you do you won't progress, or fit in, then it's probably time to reevaluate. Make sure to consider, though, exactly why it isn't working.

If you don't have much choice where you play because of age, location, or other restrictions, you can still create a challenge and find extra playing opportunities by "guesting" on other teams. Training on your own, or finding a supplementary sport, can also help you develop your overall skill and fitness level. Also, timing may result in finding different opportunities. From one year to the next, the people, and the dynamics, of a group will change. In some cases, it may not be the level of play but rather a particular team environment that isn't working for you.

Just because your local league has higher-level play and your friends are trying out, or just because your friends decide to stay put at some lower level—don't simply follow the pack. Evaluate what's good for you personally before you take the predictable road. What you do depends on what you want from the game. Ask yourself the following questions, and discuss your answers with parents, coaches, and other experienced players. Once you've determined that soccer is an activity you'll stick to, the following criteria will help you to decide what level is right for you.

1. What are your ultimate goals? High school, college, regional, and even national-level play—or fun, exercise, fitness, and enjoying the team camaraderie?

2. Do you want an organized playing environment three, four, five, or more days per week?

3. Do you have other commitments that would conflict with an increased soccer schedule?

4. Are you willing to spend extra time practicing and getting in shape on your own?

5. Do you want to spend time traveling, both to practice and to games, or to play for a local, more convenient, team?

6. How much money is your family willing to spend? (Costs go beyond team fees and equipment; travel can mean hotels and meals out.)

7. Lastly, how far are you (and your parents) willing to commute for your new team? For example, are you willing to drive more than an

hour for an hourlong practice? (In my area, you cannot join a team farther than thirty miles from where you live.)

Whatever your answers are, if you have the opportunity to move up, I suggest you ask yourself the same question many people ask when choosing a college. If you never played another minute of soccer, would you enjoy the people you are going to be with for the next few years? In the end, if you don't enjoy the people you're playing with, the team, like the college, probably won't really matter.

THE LOWDOWN ON PLAYING UP

The first time I truly focused on higher-level play was when I was sixteen. That's when I made a youth national team that had one training, in Marquette, Michigan, and my name on a certificate of congratulations. It was just a paper team, but it gave me a taste of the possibilities. Then, a little while later, on my first trip to Europe as a member of my state ODP team to play at the Gothia Cup in Sweden and the Dana Cup in Denmark, I had my first experience in a big arena. I was excited and invigorated to prove that Americans, and girls, could play, and could play well.

I didn't play every minute of every game at that tournament, but it was the highlight of my career up to that point. Looking back, I don't think the coaches thought I was spectacular. But it was a test of what kind of player I wanted to be. Not to be part of the action all the time spurred my desire to play and to improve.

The current generation of players is so much different than mine. I'm sure I would have enjoyed the sport even more (if that's possible!) if I had been shown the nuances and subtleties of the game at an even earlier age. When I was growing up, no one really even taught me the basics, such as how to strike a ball. These days, it's not unusual to find me at a clinic teaching seven-year-olds how to pass and trap the ball with the inside, outside, and instep of their feet.

Those coming onto the National Team these days had more and better training as young players and national and international playing experience at a younger age. They've been exposed to more technical soccer, and higher-level skills. Today, there are youth national teams for girls and boys at nearly all ages, beginning at fourteen. I think it's great that U.S. Soccer is dedicating itself to the development of younger players, if it's done properly, and with careful consideration for "late bloomers," who may develop into exceptional players with time. But if you've missed out on playing at a higher level, don't despair. Plenty of quality players, who went on to great college or even professional careers, didn't take the typical route. My alma mater, one of the top collegiate soccer programs in the country, both recruits players and takes talented walk-ons, as do many other programs nationwide. Some players even end up earning scholarships, although they may have never played at any select youth level. On one National Team trip, I was assigned to room with Heather Mitts. I asked her about her background. She grew up in Cincinnati, never played ODP, and ended up playing soccer at the University of Florida; she played for the WUSA and is now on the National Team.

John Ellinger is the director of youth development for U.S. Soccer and the coach of the Under 17 U.S. Men's National Team. He points out that at the younger ages in particular, maturity can radically vary within a birth year, with the older players dominating the selection process. Higher-level teams, specifically ODP, illustrate the complicated issue of development, and illustrate the need to see things in the long term and to keep things in perspective. Of Ellinger's twenty-four Under 17 players in 2004, twenty-one were born in the first six months of 1988, their birth and selection year. He claims the disparity has proven greatest in the younger years, and then begins to even out by about age sixteen. "It takes time for the younger ages to catch up, particularly in speed and size," says Ellinger, who, along with other coaches, supports creating six-month age teams in ODP in the early years.

I see it, too; Cameron has an October birthday, and among his teammates there can be a big difference between the kids with birthdays earlier in the year and those with birthdays late in the year. Whether it's due to late bloomers catching up to their peers, or finding undiscovered talent, by the end of the two-year cycle with the Under 17 team, Ellinger claims that only 60 percent of original starters in the first year make the final Under 17 roster. So if you do aspire to play in select programs, make sure you are aware of the development standards in various leagues.

Sometimes, a player is in inexperienced coaching hands, and is put on a level that may not, in the long run, serve him or her well. I did a series of clinics, and between sessions, I observed a boys' team tryout. It was an all-too-common scenario. One boy stood out from the rest. He was about four or five inches taller than the others, with legs double the size of the others. The coach doing the evaluation said to me, "He's just a beast." I asked what the boy's qualities were. "If anything comes in the air, he'll win it," the coach said. "How is his left foot?" I inquired. "He's a true lefty." "How is his right foot?" "Not so good," the coach admitted. Maybe because of his size and strength, this boy could dominate the physical aspects of the team. But perhaps he was not so capable in tight spaces or in combination plays. Maybe he didn't have as much confidence touching the ball, so in playing on this team, he avoided developing those skills and instead relied on his physical attributes. And what happens when his peers inevitably catch up to him in size? Then, he will no longer dominate. How does a good coach avoid making size and strength the boy's focus, preventing him from being pigeonholed into becoming just a tackler, and allowing him to experience the whole game? Small-sided games and touch restrictions emphasize the technical and tactical parts of the game that he may lack—but would he necessarily receive that attention?

It's always flattering to be pushed ahead, told you can make it on a better, more competitive team. But whenever you are evaluating your best possible level of play for long-term development, seek multiple opinions, and search out trustworthy experts.

CONSISTENCY, by Kristine Lilly

When I think of consistency, I think of Cal Ripkin Jr. in particular. What he accomplished in baseball is amazing. When I consider my seventeen years with the National Team, I don't think it's any one thing I've done to stay there. Of course, you take care of yourself, you stay aware of what you eat and drink, but I think everyone does that

these days. I've just gone out and played every day, and I've been fortunate to be able to do that—and in the finals of the 1999 World
Cup, when I made a crucial play, it paid off in a big way.

Of course, I'd saved the ball at pivotal moments before, but
nothing of the magnitude, and in the setting, of a World Cup final. For
the corner kicks we have our positions, and mine is on the post. In
1999, the ball came across, and I shifted with it to cover more of the
goal, in essence to make the goal area it could reach a little smaller.
When the ball was redirected on goal, my reaction was immediate—I
had to get it out of there. I headed it down, and I think Brandi actually cleared it out of the penalty area.

Other people made such a big deal of it, but the funny thing is
that I remember going to the press conference after the game where
someone asked me about heading the ball off of the line, and I had
totally forgotten about it. I was just so happy we won. I answered
that when you're in that position, you do what you have to do. Really,
any one of us in the same position would have done it. I'm just lucky
that I'm not any shorter, or any taller, or maybe I wouldn't have been
able to head that particular ball.

Because of the way the National Team was structured when I
first started, the core of us did a lot of training on our own, particularly in the winter months. Working hard was instilled in all of us. It
would make you or break you. If you had it in you, you were going to
last. And all of us did it. I think that was a huge part of creating the
core of this team.

The young kids now don't have to worry so much about going
it alone. I don't think their greater training opportunities are necessarily a negative, but I think their motivations might be more dis-
tracting, like the possibility of getting a scholarship. We worked hard
simply because we loved it.

There are definitely times I've felt burned out, but it never got
to the point where I hated playing. There are times when the work is
so hard, it might be too much. Then, I just need to get away. Any
chance I have to do that, I go to see my family. In high school, what
helped was playing other sports. I played basketball and softball in

addition to soccer. Sometimes, these days, I'll simply go out for a run or a bike ride—just to do something different.

As for my consistency, I've been fortunate to stay healthy. I've had a lingering back problem for the past four years that I'm starting to correct, and little injuries, but never anything serious, like broken bones. I'm not really sure why; maybe it's because I'm built short and stocky like my dad and my grandmother. But physical problems don't stop some people. Look at Michelle Akers, who had fourteen knee surgeries, a number of concussions, and serious chronic fatigue syndrome, and she was still amazing. Maybe it's just how you deal with it. And maybe I've handled it the right way.

MOVIN' ON UP

Many serious young athletes consider playing with older teams at one time or another. If players are mature enough and need to get more out of their team, I fully support their playing up. When I was twelve and still on the Horizon, I played with an additional team of fourteen-year-olds (although at that age, they seemed so much older). I was invited to an Under 14 tournament with this team, and I practiced with them over a couple of months. The experience was awesome. I don't know if it was because the players were physically stronger and faster and that made the level better, or if I just enjoyed the extra playing time. But I benefited either way.

While some leagues or clubs have no set restrictions, others have strict rules on playing up. For example, they require that the player rank in the top five of the team tryout. Some simply don't allow it. In any case, make sure you evaluate all the factors (such as social and emotional readiness) carefully before attempting it.

I didn't get to see Cameron play when he was very young, but I did go through a significant tryout experience with him in high school. When he started at Archbishop Mitty (where I also played soccer), he had to try out for the team. Several boys from his club team did, too. Two of them made the junior varsity team, while Cameron made the freshman team, a lower level. Obviously, this disappointed him. When Jerry asked him why he was upset, Cameron said he felt he was as good as the others, so if they made it, he should have too. Jerry was supportive, but honest. "What did you do to prepare?" he asked him, "Did you run, lift weights, put in extra time with the ball?"

"No," Cameron admitted.

"Then why do you believe you deserve to be on this team? What makes you so confident you're good enough? Remember, you have less experience and you're not as strong."

So, Cameron played for the freshman team his first year, and he had a good season. He was captain of the team, very well respected, and he got along well with the other boys. When it came time to be invited for the summer tryout for the next year's teams, he decided to work extra hard to prepare. Jerry offered him any help he might need. But Cameron worked out on his own, doing everything he could to develop himself. As a result, he made the varsity.

After his freshman year, Cameron admitted that things had worked out for the best. I asked him, "What is more important to you, playing on a team where you're not going to get a lot of time, or building a bond with the group you will be with for four years? Being with the team where you will be asked to be a leader, or going to a team where you won't really be asked your opinion, or to lead?" You can guess the answer, and I thought it was a wonderful achievement for Cameron to make that varsity team, and to be motivated to work hard for his goal. "You have only yourself to thank," I told him.

In the end, Cameron learned a great lesson by staying with the freshman squad. But it's also exciting to be pushed outside your comfort zone. Not just to practice and work so hard you can't move (which I admit people tend not to enjoy), but to be extended in a productive environment, full of energy, enthusiasm, and encouragement; to get positive reinforcement for a job well done; to move beyond a disappointment or a challenge; to decide you haven't reached your potential and put forth renewed effort. You will come back again and work hard. That effort deserves great praise. If you train hard, chances are you can earn a place on the upper echelon, but it's important that it be the right level for you.

A LEAGUE OF YOUR OWN

From choosing a school to finding a doctor, the more carefully you do your soccer homework, the better your chance of finding the right level. Contact the administrators and coaches of the program, or of the league—both the one you are already a part of, and the one to which you are thinking of moving. Ask them for advice and referrals of those involved with their program.

If it is comfortable, get the opinion of your current coach. Talk to the players on the prospective team, as well as graduates of the program. Speak with other families about the commitment—time and money. Don't be reluctant to ask for all sides—the good, the bad, and the ugly. Ask about the stress level and the focus on winning. Check out the Internet. Many times various leagues will post information on their program, and other soccer Web sites can also give you relevant information.

Observe various teams in a game, but, more important, watch their practice. And watch both practice and games more than once. If you observe a couple of times, you will see the team doing different things; or take notice that they train and play a game in the same style. Both scenarios offer useful information. (If you see them before game day, they may be doing tactics or a walk-through. That's why you'll get a more complete picture if you come to more than one event.) Ask to guest play. Try both training and games. Finally, take your time. Start your homework early so you can consider everything carefully before deciding.

Even in today's competitive youth sports arena, sometimes it's better to take it one step at a time, and not to worry about advancing too fast. But if you feel you're ready, don't be intimidated. Just boost your confidence, and be prepared to try your hardest, whatever level you choose.

chapter eleven: train hard, win easy

There are classic strategies that soccer players have used since Game One, but to see them executed by the best players in the world is still magic to me. For example, the Brazilian great Ronaldo has more moves than a bag full of snakes, and the nuances of his game always bring me back to the basics. When Ronaldo eludes a defender with a wall pass, there's nothing standard about his play: Every touch he makes is precise; he throws the defender off balance with a beautiful little shimmy and bursts past him with the speed of an Olympic sprinter. Watching Ronaldo in the World Cup, I saw him transform a simple give-and-go play into poetry—and was transported back in time to when I first learned how effective that simple tactic can be.

I was fourteen, and a member of the Under 16 ODP Northern California State team. It was a long drive to practice, and when my mom saw the cows lying down in the fields along the way, she said it was a sign of rain. Sure enough, it turned into a cold, wet day, with lots of mud. Training was divided into two three-hour sessions; the day's theme was combination play, so the coach had us spend the entire time doing wall passes. A wall pass— also called a "give-and-go" or a "one-two"—is a one-touch return pass to a player who runs into an open space to receive the ball back; it's like bouncing a ball off a wall. For six hours—first in the wet grass, and eventually in the mud—we worked one-twos in every conceivable format: around cones, in pairs, in small-sided games, and then in full scrimmages. During the course of the session, we'd periodically give that impatient "I've got it already" kind of look.

Particularly when you're starting out, long practice sessions can be counterproductive, this day was actually an economical training. It offered not only the technical skill breakdown—when to pass, which part of the foot to use, how much to dribble—but the tactical field awareness as well—where and when to run, what to do if you don't get the ball, and so forth. It was the first time soccer had been broken down for me into such small parts, and despite the eye rolling and dramatic sighs, it dawned on me how much I enjoyed the details of the game, especially dissecting this elementary skill, then having it finally come together.

After that, just as I feel watching Ronaldo, I was invigorated; I could have done wall passes the whole weekend. That day turned into one of my most memorable youth training sessions. With that dedication to practicing the wall pass, we became the best at doing it of any team in our age group in the area, and our fundamental play improved greatly.

Not everybody feels this way, but I love practice. Don't get me wrong, I love games, too. But practice is my bread and butter; it's where the game starts for me, with that day-in and day-out opportunity to hone my skills in a free, even experimental environment. Once the routine takes hold, I enjoy the application of what I've learned, even if it's just 3 v 3 drills. I get totally involved—breaking the moves down, and doing them over and over. Practicing the same moves in a defined space opens a window on the subtleties of the game. I can't get enough.

At my level, I think my teammates and I all enjoy practice. But like everyone, we have our days. Some sessions, I feel as if I'm walking on air; I'm in the zone. Other times, I'm tired or sore, or distracted by something weighing on my mind. Over time, I'm conditioned to build an adaptive mechanism, to overcome a bad patch, to push forward and ride it through.

Since soccer is interactive in nature, practice is also social. When I'm with the National Team, we're like every other team, kidding around. In some drills we divide up and wear different-colored pinnies, and if Julie gets the green ones, she does this goofy chant she perfected as a high school cheerleader (and homecoming queen, by the way): "Nah, nah, nah, nobody messes with the green machine." We all laugh, and, of course, everyone wants to kill her team. "The green team's going down!" we shout. We get ourselves amped up in this way, and that lends itself to a team spirit that even carries over into game time.

Unfortunately for some, there's a stigma attached to learning—that it shouldn't be fun. If we do enjoy the process of learning, then we think that what we picked up can't be as valuable as those things that weren't such fun to learn. It's basically a misconception that fun and learn ing can't and shouldn't go together. But my greatest soccer education has come about when I was having the most fun, and I'm determined to keep it that way. That's why, when I do a clinic, I make sure I convey to the kids that our plan is to learn, and to have a good time doing so. In the classroom, on the field, and at home, you should always try to combine pleasure and learning in a practical, useful fashion. In that kind of atmosphere, the lessons are absorbed most naturally, and most effectively.

When I'm tired or having a rough day, I use practice as a spring-board to lift up my spirits. I look for a teammate who is in good form, and raring to go. I warm up passing with her, and we chat. This often helps to jump-start me and reshape my attitude. Then, I also get myself out of a funk by beginning practice with a simple mantra: Focus on something simple. So I'll start with short passes, for example, to gain my confidence and recharge my batteries.

Sometimes, though, I'm tired or low, and there's just no way to get over it. Not every day is going to be great, nor can I get out of every funk. I get through by focusing on what the coach is asking me to do, and I vow that the next day I'll come back to try to get the job done better. But if a parent sees a child in a blue mood, and she doesn't seem to want to pick it up, maybe it's the best option on some days just to let it go. Even Ronaldo probably has his down days.

PRACTICE MAKES PERFECT

In a ninety-minute game, each player touches the ball an average of only two to three minutes total. Practice is the place to get maximum time on the ball, and to refine skills. Particularly for developing players (even those up through college) it's critical to get a good foundation of functional, technical training, with the tactics built in. When young players ask me how a practice drill fits into playing, I remind them that 3 v 1 keep-away games, or small-sided possession games, are miniature pictures of the entire field. I also use the example of juggling, when you use different parts of your body to keep the ball in the air. I don't use juggling in a game very often, but when the ball comes to my thigh, I know what it will feel like, and how to control it.

Growing up, I learned about the importance of hard work off the field as well. When I was a teenager and my mom couldn't find someone to work for one of her vendors, she'd corral my brother and me. For eight hours a shift, we would be on our feet handing out food samples in a supermarket. It was hard work, but I took a lot of pride in the money I earned. When I was young, my brother and I each had a bank account. For my young fans who don't know, back in those days, you brought your bankbook along and handed it to the teller, and the teller stamped it with a record of your deposits. Dollar by dollar, I faithfully saved, excited to see how much interest I was earning. It was an investment in the future, like daily soccer training.

Sometimes hard work is a grind, but there's something rewarding about gritting your teeth and getting through it. There can even be pleasure in the grind, if you're convinced the work will make you better. While I've been writing this book, we've also been getting ready for the Olympics, and I'm just finishing a period of very intense training with the National Team. In up to three sessions a day (two for soccer, one for weight lifting), we were pushed to the max. At the end of each day, I literally had to drag myself home. It was a major effort just to walk up the steps; my muscles ached. I was physically and mentally exhausted. But I knew I was getting better, and the team was getting better—and that we were increasing our chance to go for the gold.

After a good night's sleep, I would return to the field and feel renewed. That's the nature of training; it makes you adaptive. You go through cycles of stress and rest, which increases your performance threshold (not to mention improving your cardiovascular fitness and general conditioning). After all, that's why you do it. But these cycles also require that you sometimes defer satisfaction: At the time of this writing the Olympics are still weeks away. Just like those old bankbooks taught me, I recognize that I have to make an investment today if I want to collect interest later on.

Sometimes it's hard for inexperienced players to see the correlation between training and games. After all, the game has all the great facets: uniforms, referees, spectators on the sidelines, the score. Young players always want to know why we don't just get better by playing games. But practice is necessary for improving skills, developing strategy, and building a team. Wearing those pinnies gets you ready to change into a uniform, and games are where you ultimately fit together the pieces of what you do in practice. When it comes time to play a game, you have access to all the information you have been saturated with in practice.

For that reason, practice is often loaded with repetition, so you can absorb the skills. Practice breaks things down into smaller parts, which you can't do in a game. Soccer has two forty-five-minute halves and no time-outs for strategizing or mulling things over. It's not like football, baseball, or even basketball, in which you can come together for a little discussion while the clock is running. The minute you try to dissect what's going on, it's too late. Practice creates the mosaic of the thousands of skills, runs, and decisions you learn and perfect so they become second nature. With extensive practice, in a game, you instantly recall and perform the drills without missing a beat.

When the Dutch star Ruud van Nistelrooy found himself in the eighteen-yard box at the near post with a defender draped over him in the Union of European Football Association (UEFA) Euro 2004 Championships in Portugal, he had not a millisecond of doubt about how to put his body in a position to score a goal on an acrobatic, and exquisite, side volley. He knew how to make that run; how to fight to get in front of the defender; where to be in relation to the near post; how not to swing too hard, or insert the slightest extra movement—all because he had done every piece of that move thousands of times before in practice.

For the young players reading this, you should realize that to be great, your practice has to be lifelong. No one really ever stops needing the work: Ask Zinedine Zidane or Mia Hamm if you don't believe me. Obviously, to be considered one of the most skillful players in the world—who was so crucial in helping France win the 1998 World Cup—Zidane didn't get that way in his sleep. And Mia, the highest goal scorer in international women's soccer, still works on finishing every day in practice. I'm in the same boat. In fact, before the Olympics the coaches of the National Team talked to me about my need to improve 1 v 1 defending, and together we decided that, whenever possible, ten minutes before or after every training, I would practice with a couple of attacking players, letting them dribble right at me as I concentrated on my footwork, balance, judgment, and patience. At other times I need to do different things. For example, just yesterday, our last training on U.S. soil before heading off for the 2004 Olympics, I worked on long balls with Kate Markgraf. And during a recent scrimmage, April, our coach, walked over to my side of the field and gave me pointers while I played.

It's not any different than Mia working on her shooting. "Watch this," she said to Joy and me one day recently at practice. She shot ball after ball, all of them flying over the post. We told her what we were seeing, and she made slight adjustments. She groomed her shot and eventually found her rhythm.

Practice is most effective if you're surrounded by players who are better than you, at least in certain areas. But one of the nice things about practice is that like a wall pass it can involve a lot of give-and-take. Mia is a great goal scorer, and Julie has a savvy understanding of the midfield, so playing against them forces me to improve. And like Mia asking us to evaluate her shot, working together helps us all to be on the top of our game.

If I could offer any advice to players who really want to raise their level of play, I'd say always put yourself in situations in which you are teetering on the edge of success or failure, so you won't be afraid of a challenge in the game. In a game situation, you may not want to take certain risks, because a result is on the line. Practice is the best time to take the chances that come with honing your skills. In one of my clinics we were doing a drill in which I was trying to get kids to embrace the fact that soccer is a contact sport. I asked everyone to get a partner, but one of the smallest girls didn't find one. So I became her partner. She looked up at me with these big eyes, questioning how she was going to go against me. We battled while she managed to shield the ball for a few seconds, getting better each time she tried it. If she had been paired with a smaller player, she likely wouldn't have explored the art of shielding, footwork, or balance— let alone the sense of confidence and satisfaction she got from going up against a bigger, stronger player.

When I practice with my stepson, I'm always impressed by the strides made in coaching and skills development. Cameron, who plays for the Silicon Valley Football Club in California, is coached by Jeff Baicher, who played college soccer at Santa Clara and professionally in the MLS. When I take part in their trainings, they're as good as any I've ever done. It's not as if the players simply float around the field; the mantra is that every touch and every run has a purpose. Jeff teaches the guys the fine points, like how to use their bodies and change directions. Of course, they're still young and sometimes overly aggressive or self-centered (dribbling can be fun), or a bit naïve in their play, but their strength and their speed of play is impressive, and Jeff asks them to think quicker, make better decisions, and see the field.

PRACTICING SOLO

It's amazing how much more technical and organized soccer training is now. When I was growing up, we practiced twice a week (three times when I got older) and played one game on the weekend, unless there was a tournament, and I didn't start playing in tournaments until I was eleven. Today, with year-round soccer (which I didn't play until I was nearly in college), there are an incredible number of games being played. Too many in my opinion (but that's another story).

Children in sports are often overly organized. Informal play gives them the opportunity to be independent, creative, and self-motivated. They dictate the place, the time, the rules, and the structure—or lack of it. When I was young, aside from formal practice, I was out on my front lawn every day, juggling or kicking a ball. I'd play with the neighborhood kids or my brother. He and I often took it into the house, playing 1 v 1 in our hallway, which couldn't have been more than three feet wide. (Of course, that would drive our mother crazy.) Even today, I'm always looking for ways to fit in informal training. I'll head to my local field for a pickup game, or join Cameron and four of his buddies and make up a practice session.

That said, these casual skills sessions don't have to last for hours—even fifteen minutes a day of juggling or footwork can be a significant addition when compounded over time. Mix it up with friends, or play a little by yourself. What's important is that you develop the habit, and put the fun into it, the way we do with the National Team. We play informal games and create challenges against one another all the time. The rewards are simple, but satisfying, like the losers serving the winners lunch and busing their trays in the cafeteria at the Home Depot Center, buying coffee or smoothies, or hitting the ground for push-ups and sit-ups while the winners gloat.

720

Try this ultimate challenge. It's called a 720, and here's why. Using these 12 ball-juggling surfaces (laces / instep of both feet, outside of the feet, inside of the feet, thighs, chest, shoulders, head) and keeping the ball up in the air, use as many of those surfaces as you can in 60 seconds. Multiply the number of surfaces you successfully use (at least once), by the number of seconds you keep the ball up. (Your maximum score would be $12 \times 60 = 720$.)

SURVIVAL OF THE FITTEST

Aside from practice sessions and organized soccer, the current emphasis on conditioning, even in youth sports, is miles ahead of where it was when I was young. When my dad started coaching, he didn't know soccer from volleyball. He did know calisthenics and running because he had been a Marine, so we practiced that. "Take two laps around the field," he would tell us. We did leg lifts, push-ups, and sit-ups. Then, for the soccer practice, he put out some cones and we dribbled around them, and we played some small-sided games.

That was it in the old days. Now, some supplementary training is critical to the overall development (and protection from injury) of soccer players, and, most likely, of all serious youth athletes. The sport has so many different physical requirements that stamina, agility, flexibility, and explosiveness all benefit from attention off the field, particularly in this era of ambitious goals and playing schedules. If you don't have the time necessary to do weight work or plyometrics (explosiveness and agility work), a knowledgeable coach can build these elements into soccer practice. (Also, you can learn to incorporate some of them independently into your routine. The Internet has plenty of suggestions for this training as well, but always consult an expert first, of course.)

Some young athletes and their families feel compelled to sign up for extra strength and fitness courses, or even to hire personal trainers. But you don't have to take this route. Strength and fitness has a cumulative effect. Basically, it's building a habit by maintaining a steady routine that counts. Particularly in the beginning, even a few minutes a day devoted to some form of conditioning and flexibility (stretching) is a good supplement to your soccer. You can build from there. Again, you can learn these exercises from an experienced coach, or in consultation with an expert.

Ironically, my first introduction to fitness training was from Jack LaLanne (no doubt a name only the older readers of this book will recognize!), whom I used to watch on TV with my mom in the mornings. Today, the fitness guru is still in tremendous shape at age eighty-nine. I learned to do pull-ups, push-ups, and sit-ups, which we still do in the weight room with the National Team three days a week. But I think even Jack may be a little intimidated if he saw the rest of our routine. We also do speed and form training twice a week. This is technical running in which you learn to get the most power and explosion from each step, including working on various directions and footwork.

I began lifting weights my senior year in high school, and it became a regular routine by college. When I realized that focusing on weights made me so much stronger and helped rebuild and prevent injuries (particularly after my first ACL injury), I became devoted to it.

Before I started strength training, all I could think about was, Am I in the right position on the field? What can I do with the ball? What's the next play? Strength was a whole new dimension. Soccer was just soccer until it became part of an entire training routine, and until I became stronger and saw how that strength helped me on the field. Strength training became my ally.

PUTTING PRACTICE INTO PLAY

How do you play when you're losing? How do you hold on when you're winning? What do you do when you're down, with ten minutes left to play? Putting yourself in these situations in practice most accurately duplicates the challenges of a game; the experiences in practice build your confidence so you'll know what to do when you face them for real. You physically and mentally rehearse a comeback, or holding on to a lead, and that gives you a reference to go back to during a game. I assure you, it works.

If you work on runs in the box in practice, for example, you'll execute them much better in the game. Most of the time, players have only a handful of opportunities, if they're lucky, to get in behind a winded defender or cross the ball and get it into the box. Late in a game, good preparation shows up in your ability to make those runs and crosses—and beat those defenders (which is why I believe in hard work, too). So if you only go through the motions during training, you likely won't be prepared to pull it off in the ninetieth minute when the game may be on the line.

I count on the coach to lead me through training that is designed to prepare me for the game. Good training has a progression, with individual learning that transitions to work for the team as a whole, and then, to gamelike situations. That's why most practices, no matter what the age of the players, should end in a scrimmage—as a reward, and to allow players to enact in game scenarios what they've learned in training.

On the National Team, we recently practiced a potential comeback situation in which we changed our formation—pushing the defense up high, going from a four back to a three back—so we were more aggressively pushing forward. Sure enough, we changed to that formation near the end of our next game against the Under 17 boys. We forced them to give away the ball in their own defending third, and Lindsey Tarpley scored in literally the final minute to tie the score, 1–1.

THE TRUE GOAL OF COMPETITION

Youth sports have become like the stock market. At the end of the day, it seems that the bottom line is all that counts. And the question all too often is not, "Did you get better?" or "Did you have fun?" but rather, "Did you win?" Quite simply, usually the only thing people construe as success is a victory.

In the inner circles of youth sports, you often hear that development is being sacrificed for winning. Can using early physical maturity (size, speed, strength), specializing in one position at an early age, or going with a lineup that severely limits playing time for some result in a winning team? No doubt it can. But sacrificing education in the basics of the game (the optimal window of skill development is ages eight to twelve, when children are most capable of learning new patterns of movement), not giving every player a chance to experiment and to learn, results in severely shortchanging all young athletes—ironically, even those who are pushed ahead.

Whacking a ball long to a physically dominant player who stuffs it into the goal may get the job done, but it doesn't build lasting success. At the highest levels, every player on the field has to have some degree of finesse. Take Cindy Parlow. Although I'm sure she used her size to her advantage when she was young (and still does) what sets her apart are her amazing ball-handling skills. She brings the whole package: She can dominate in the air with her size, but she can also deliver devastating crosses, take defenders on 1 v 1, and volley in a shot with the best of them.

At the other end of the spectrum are players like Kristine Lilly, who has refined her ball shielding and dribbling skills to the point where her relatively small size is unimportant. I just love watching her slalom through a crowd of spellbound defenders. Coaches and players have to realize that, in the end, size is not the deciding factor in success at elite levels of play, and they have to begin to focus on the subtle aspects of the game.

In 2004, U.S. Soccer put out a document entitled "Lessons Learned from the 2003 Women's World Cup and How to Apply them to the Youth Game." The introduction read, in part, "Across the USA, we must continue to place technical development as our first priority. We need coaches to commit to the full technical development of their players, by deemphasizing winning and reemphasizing the importance of technical sophistication with the ball." If it were not for that emphasis, our team would be particularly challenged against physically imposing sides like those of Norway, Germany, and Nigeria. Technical ability and team play beat physical prowess almost every time.

From every corner of the country, experts decry the overemphasis on winning at an early age. Brett Thompson is the director of coaching for the Ohio South Youth Soccer Association, a Region II ODP women's program staff member, a native-born American, and former high-level player in England, where he spent his youth. He writes that in Ohio (and in most states), many players start select play at eight or nine years old, that they are being scouted and identified by age six or seven, and that they play a total of about eighty games per year (outdoor and indoor). By contrast, professional teams in Europe play no more than sixty-four, and never more than two games per week, let alone the five games per weekend that young people typically play these days in tournaments. Writes Thompson, "Where does the player development come from if players are playing three games a week? How can teams practice if all they are doing is playing to survive and stay in the division they are in or trying to move up? It becomes the human instinct of survival and as a result coaches play to win rather than develop."

John Ellinger, director of youth development for U.S. Soccer and coach of the boy's Under 17 National Team concurs, and laments the emphasis on going for the "quick fix" win. "Some coaches can't get past this, but coaches who have enough confidence and understanding know that in time, maturity evens out, and that the developmental system will work." Ellinger speaks for the girl's side as well. He is in his third year of coaching his daughter's team, now Under 12, where he fights to stem the tide. "Win or lose, I play each of the eighteen girls at least half a game."

Even at the highest levels, there is time set aside for development.

In the first half of the season at Santa Clara, Jerry tells his players the goal is to attempt in a game what they do in training. He isn't so concerned with the outcome and the score. All recruited freshmen play, and start during the first half of the season. His goal is to give all his players an opportunity, and also to discover what works best for the team so that the ideal is eventually created. Of course, the ultimate goal is to peak at the appropriate time, and to win, but equally important is the message that is communicated about the importance of development.

I am amazed that going for the "quick fix" happens on such a wide scale, especially at the younger age levels. There is so much exploration that should be part of a sports education that is not necessarily about results. Besides, what's the point of winning? Getting a trophy? You can buy a trophy or a ribbon for a few dollars. A better ranking or entry into a top tournament? Is that really so important? If you want to be seen, or want to succeed on a higher level, you can get there. Ultimately, an experienced coach with a good set of eyes will find you.

I feel sympathetic to the many well-meaning youth coaches who want to develop players but are under pressure from those paying their salaries to "produce results," defined, of course, as a winning record. I emphatically urge both parents and players to gain an understanding of this issue, and to scope out and choose a team that stresses player development. If you properly hone your game, there will be plenty of opportunities in the future to fill your trophy case.

DEALING WITH VICTORY AND DEFEAT

For a committed athlete, winning and losing carry the weight of the world. The investment is not just physical but psychological and emotional. But there's no shame in that, either, if you ask me. I remember looking at a picture of the awards ceremony after the 2000 Olympics. There we were, standing on the podium with our silver medals around our necks. You could tell by our faces how each of us was dealing with it. Nikki Serlenga had her mouth open, looking dumbfounded. Julie was staring straight in front of her, her hands on her hips, with an "I'm not finished" expression.

(When we were on the *Tonight Show* with Jay Leno, and the 2000 Olympics was mentioned, Julie quipped that it was where we won "white gold.") I was smiling as I stood on that podium. I wasn't being flippant. It was a big deal after all, but I also thought we played really hard and did a great job. We just fell short by one goal. There are those who hate losing, and maybe you'd call them poor sports. There are those who have it in perspective, and others ask, "Couldn't they take it more seriously?" Judging from that photo, I'm somewhere in the middle.

Obviously, we're going to the 2004 Olympics to win. At the elite level, that's our primary responsibility. But 2004 is my third Olympics, and I think my more relaxed, mature perspective will help me both to win, and to savor the experience. And I don't think it's unreasonable for young players to find a balance—to swallow a hard loss if they must, but to take the enjoyment and lessons from the event at the same time, the kind that become part of the good memories.

For the U.S. National Team, we've been on both sides of the win-loss column in big games. After winning the inaugural Women's World Cup in China in 1991, we suffered a bitter defeat to Norway in the 1995 Women's World Cup in Sweden. Our historic victory in 1999, the closest thing imaginable to a perfect win, was again followed by a disheartening loss in 2003. That's simply the nature of sports. We can't celebrate the sweetness of that victory without the contrasting bitter taste of defeat.

It's harder to be philosophical when you've gotten close but missed your goal. I've been to the Olympics, but I never got to an NCAA final. We almost did in my senior year of college when Santa Clara was the number-one-ranked team in the country. The memory is as clear as yesterday for me now. We hadn't lost a game. We were dominating in the semifinals of the National Championships, up against Connecticut 1–0. With ten seconds left, a Connecticut player took a wild and desperate shot from about thirty-five yards out. But it had just enough pace to beat our goalkeeper, skipping right through her legs. It sputtered, barely crossing the line, but it tied the game. No one scored in overtime, so we went to PKs. Each team had a miss, leaving us tied. So we kept going, until our team missed on our sixth shot. It was heartbreaking. We were so close.

The vision of that game has lasted my whole career. As painful as it still is, I try hard to use the memory to my advantage. I thought about it years later while playing against China in the fateful 1999 World Cup final, to keep me on my toes. As the game was winding down in a scoreless tie, it was almost like a repeat. But I tried to hold up through my physical and mental fatigue. I had learned in that college game what can happen if you let down, since I feel our team gave up in those final seconds. I did lots of self-talk (assuring or instructing by talking to myself), chatting out loud constantly, reminding myself to stay in the game and make each play carefully—to keep it simple, to try hard not to let down and make a mistake—telling myself not to give away an easy pass or to lose possession. I feel sure that my bitter experience with Santa Clara prepared me to focus that day through my fatigue.

I've learned over time that you don't get to some divine place of accepting your losses overnight. I've been dealing with both wonderful successes and some real lows for over twenty five years. Over time, they tend to counterbalance each other. I find the best way to survive is to try to stay in the middle emotionally. That's because time and again, you see the consequences in sports of not keeping this balance.

One of the first things I learned about losing is not to overreact to the emotion of the moment. My style is to have a very positive recap of the game—after the dust settles, of course. I once coached an Under 16 club team in Northern California that qualified for the U.S. Youth Soccer Regional Championships, a competition among the State Championship teams, in this case in the West. We got to the semifinals, and lost to a Colorado team in PKs. The team was exhausted, which made the loss more devastating. After everyone shook hands, I high-fived the players coming off the field. We came together, and I told them how proud I was of their effort and of the fact that they never quit. I often wonder why some coaches tell their team that their effort was not good enough, that they failed. Once the game is over, there's nothing we can do to change the outcome. Negativity only beats the players down and robs them of acknowledging their efforts.

On the flipside, I feel strongly that when you win, you should celebrate. You don't have to rub your opponents' noses in it, but victory legitimizes all the training and sacrifice that carry you through a season. All you have to do is look at my face on the book cover to recognize I'm a big advocate of celebration! But while you savor the victory, you should try to learn from it just as much as you do from a loss. You put in effort, and you are rewarded. You continue to remember all the things you did well in the games you win so you can try to put them all together for the next game, even though you have the understanding that because every game is different—opponent, surface, referee—so, too, can the outcome vary.

One of the best ways I know to learn is to keep a diary of your games, your practices, and your progress toward goals. When you sit down to write after a breather from the game, the emotions of winning or losing aren't as immediate, and you can mentally map out what went right and wrong. There's a diary on my nightstand. I go back over it and use it as a learning tool. I write down how I was feeling during training, if I had a good day, or feel I need work in specific areas. I record whether I have accomplished my goals. It's important to do this for both practice and games, to see if what you have been doing in training translates to competition.

Every day, I set out four goals I want to accomplish for myself in a practice or a game. In practice, I write them down if they're very important, or stuck in my mind. For a game, I always write them down before I play to solidify them in my mind. My most recent, for example, reads: communicate better with the team; work on the outside of my left foot; make more runs to get into positive positions in the attack; tackle hard and low to keep balance. If I attempt each of these in practice at least once (hopefully more), whether or not I am successful, I have met my expectations for the day. While winning and losing aren't always in my control, I understand that it's always up to me to get the most the out of my experience on the field.

Grandfather Knows Best: At age five, sitting on my grandfather's lap with my brother, Chad. "Gagi" used to give me $1 for every goal; $1.50 for an assist, to show me the importance of helping others, and he did that for me straight through college. Unfortunately, his prices never went up. (Brandi Chastain)

My Idea of Playing Dirty: Here I am, at age thirteen, after a youth club game. We may have not been the best team, but we were definitely the muddiest. (Brandi Chastain)

The Thrill of Victory: I was always known for my theatrical celebrations. Here I am after scoring a goal in the high school sectional final. During my four years at Archbishop Mitty, we were the three-time Central Coast Section champions. Notice I kept my jersey on back then. (Brandi Chastain)

Gimme a B . . . : Yes, my mother used to be a cheerleader. How else to explain her patrolling the sidelines of my youth games with a megaphone, even though there were only a dozen people in attendance. Years later, at the 1999 World Cup final, I could actually hear her cheering among the ninety thousand fans. And she didn't need a megaphone. *(Brandi Chastain)*

All-American Girl: With my teammate Linda Hoffman on the eve of the 1989 NCAA championships, when we were undefeated and ranked number one in the country. *(Brandi Chastain)*

No Guts, No Glory: During the 1996 Olympic semifinal against Norway, I tore my MCL, and when I came out, then assistant coach April Heinrichs encouraged me to go back in if I could handle the pain. "You're better with one leg than most people are with two," she told me at half time. (Note: Although sometimes pros play hurt, I do *not* recommend it in the youth game.) *(JohnTodd/ www.internationalsportsimages.com)*

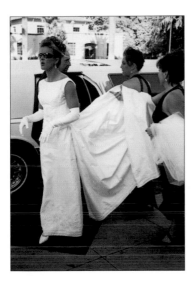

My Future's So Bright: Wearing sunglasses on my wedding day. They don't call me Hollywood for nothing. *(Brandi Chastain)*

Female Bonding: Before you can reach the summit of the soccer world, you need to learn how to work as a team. Here we are with our coach Tony DiCicco (with mustache) before the 1999 World Cup, getting ready to climb to the top of the world. *(Brandi Chastain)*

O Say, Can You Sing? I was belting out the National Anthem so loudly at the gold medal ceremonies of the 1996 Olympics, I was practically yelling. My favorite part is "home of the brave." It reminds me of the way we are on the soccer field. *(JohnTodd/ www.internationalsportsimages.com)*

The Shot Seen 'Round the World: "Do you want to take a penalty kick?" asked Coach Tony DiCiccio after 120 scoreless minutes in the 1999 Women's World Cup final against China. I told him I was ready. "Will you take it with your left foot?" "Yes," I answered confidently. You know the rest. *(Robert Beck/*Sports Illustrated*)*

Lethal Weapons: Leading up to the 1999 World Cup, I worked hard on strength and conditioning with trainer Dave Oliver. Still, my stepson, Cameron, always jokes about my arms: "Are those things registered?" he'll ask. *(Brandi Chastain)*

The House That Brandi Built: I was more nervous throwing out the first pitch at Yankee Stadium than I was taking that penalty kick against China in the 1999 World Cup. I was literally hyperventilating, and I told Joe Torre I was going to pitch like El Duque. "Well," said Torre, "you better not throw it in the dirt or they'll boo you." I got it over the plate.
(Brandi Chastain)

Air Chastain: When the First Family visited us in the locker room after our victory in the 1999 World Cup, it was the ultimate exclamation point to a perfect day. Mrs. Clinton invited the team to go on Air Force 1 to Cape Canaveral with some other high-profile women, including two U.S. senators, to visit a female astronaut. It's the only way to fly.
(Brandi Chastain/Official White House Photograph)

Tigress Woods? Following the 1999 World Cup, I got to play golf with the man himself (and my brother, Chad) in San Francisco. Tiger called my parents from the course and joked, "I'm out here with Chad and your other son." *(Brandi Chastain)*

A League of Our Own: I fought my whole career to have a women's professional league, which made winning the first WUSA championship in 2001 that much sweeter. *(John Todd/www.internationalsportsimages.com)*

The Family That Plays Together . . . : I often join my stepson, Cameron, and his buddies at soccer practice. Here we are after a session with my husband and Cameron's dad, Jerry. *(Gloria Averbuch)*

Look, Ma, No Cavities: Mia Hamm and I were hanging with a friend, who is a dentist, and we found this giant toothbrush—which is just about the right size for Julie Foudy's mouth. *(Brandi Chastain)*

The Way Too Fab Four: Striking a pose with my housemates, Kristine Lilly, Julie Foudy, and Mia Hamm, before a Madonna concert. Julie dubbed our place Villa Viejas (house of the old ladies), and also, Four Chicks and an Elevator. *(Brandi Chastain)*

We're No Angels: For a Bud Light commercial, Julie Foudy and I donned mink coats and wigs to portray soccer-playing crime fighters. We caught the perpetrators by kicking balls at them. By the way, I'm Farrah Fawcett; Julie is Kate Jackson—as if you couldn't tell. *(Brandi Chastain)*

The Beautiful Game: Win, lose, or draw, always keep smiling. *(John Todd/ www.internationalsportsimages.com)*

Going Out in Style: From Athens, Georgia, where we won our first gold medal, to Athens, Greece, where the 91ers played together for the last time, I've learned that winning isn't everything but it sure is fun. *(AP Photo/Kevork Djansezian)*

chapter twelve: the 110-percent solution

"Why am I doing this?" That question often went through my mind while waiting for the six A.M. bus that took me through Berkeley and Oakland on my way to Lake Merritt Junior College for an eight A.M. class. The previous year, I had enrolled at the University of California at Berkeley. But I didn't do well academically my first semester, and I found myself on probation. My second-semester grades were improving until I got sidelined by my first ACL tear and had to go through surgery and rehabilitation. With the distraction and time taken off for my injury, I did miserably in my classes, ended up with some incompletes, and, basically, got kicked out of prestigious U.C. Berkeley.

I was told I could go to junior college, complete the classes, and come back. Hence, my long commutes to Lake Merritt Junior College. I went through a lot of soul searching on those long mornings.

I had always considered myself a good student—I wasn't going to get 1600 on the SATs, but I enjoyed going to class and learning. Still, like many college freshmen, I was on my own for the first time. I had to make decisions about how I was going to spend my time: what to eat, when to go to bed, and how many hours to study. Sometimes, there were eight hundred people in a class. Oh, they won't miss me if I don't go, I told myself. So I didn't. And every day I skipped left me further and further behind. I neglected my studies until eventually there was no coming back and, then, having essentially failed out, I was paying the price.

It was a big lesson in effort for me—if I'd actually made an honest effort and prepared for my classes at Berkeley I could have avoided my suspension and gotten a degree. When you find you're good at something, the way I was at soccer, and things come easily, you can often get by, even excel, without a lot of hard work. But college required focusing at a whole new level. I couldn't simply say, as I did about attending class, I'll do it tomorrow. Like a young athlete intent on playing up, I was finding my own academic level.

It took me a while to find an approach that worked, which reminds me of a story that Colleen Hacker, the sports psychologist for the women's National Team, once told us. Two men are asked to chop down two trees within a certain amount of time. They are equal in strength, and have identical axes, but what they don't have in common is their approach to getting the job done. One quickly picks up the axe and begins to chop and chop, exhausting himself. Instead of diving in headfirst, the other man sits back, thinks about the task, and maps out his plan. He spends more time preparing, thinking, and sharpening his axe so it can cut more deeply with every stroke, so that when he begins to chop, it is easy for him to complete the job. Colleen uses this story as an example of how to prepare for games, but the lesson is one that I think works just as well off the field.

For me, the willingness to prepare, and the understanding of preparation, is more than half the battle. That is what sets apart the good from the average, and the great from the good. Initially, I thought since I did well in high school, everything would work out fine in college. But I didn't quite understand what I was getting into, and that the work would be so much more challenging. I didn't do my homework; I cut class; I failed out. In other words, I paid for being a bad planner and for being ill prepared.

After leaving U.C. Berkeley and junior college, I decided I would come home and go to the local junior college, West Valley, in San Jose, in order to transfer to Santa Clara. I had to retake some courses, since some of the credits I had acquired weren't transferable to Santa Clara. At first, I felt defeated not only because I had been booted from Berkeley and had to come back home, but also because I had to redo some of the college work. For a long time, I thought that I would never find my way out of this slump, that I would be perpetually stuck in a maze. I wanted so badly to advance, but at least initially, it felt as if I was standing still. It didn't help that I was also still getting over my second ACL injury.

It turned out, though, that I got much more involved in those classes when I did them over, when I was more prepared, and when I appreciated them far more. That sense of appreciation deepened in 1991, after the World Cup, and not quite in the way you might expect. In 1991, I hadn't quite finished Santa Clara because I took time off school for that event, so I had to pay for an additional semester. That's private school tuition, and it isn't cheap. I had earned this money myself, and believe me, I wanted every teacher to come to class on time and to be prepared. I wanted my fellow students to be on the ball and as ready as I was. If a professor tried to end class early, I got upset. Studying was simply practice for class, class practice for tests, and tests the drill that would get me my degree. By the time I got my degree in television and communications, I was as committed to my education as I was to soccer.

Anyone who has ever faced a challenge, and conquered it, will not be surprised when I say that it's the hardest-fought victories, those that require the most preparation and work, that are the most satisfying. My college degree felt that way for me.

IF AT FIRST YOU FAIL, TRY, TRY AGAIN

My soccer career has also made me understand the value of effort. At a soccer convention in 1989, Jerry conducted a session on defending, and used me to demonstrate. He did some drills, and I was trying as hard as I could. Then, in front of the room of coaches, he stopped me and said, "Now, everyone, what you've just seen is an example of what you *don't* want in defending." He had me step out and brought in another player from our team, Tami Batista, to show how to do it right.

Jerry was shocked at how poor my defending was. My technique wasn't good; my decision making was poor. He says that in retrospect he feels very bad for embarrassing me in public. But as uncomfortable as it was, I knew it was true. I was great at scoring, but as can be the case with forwards, I didn't put forth as much effort for defending. Some coaches would have found that acceptable, but not Jerry. He calls his a "blue-collar" program, one that relies on every single player putting in as much effort when she doesn't have the ball as when she does. For Jerry, the right way to play is to put in an honest day's work. I don't mind when coaches "tell it like it is." I just want to get better, and that was Jerry's goal for me, too.

Ironically, when I wanted to get back on the National Team after my stint in Japan, the coaches told me there was only one way to make the team again—become a defender. They wanted to change the type of players in the back, from man-to-man markers, with no responsibility on the ball, to a zone, with the backs commanding an area. Despite my clinic experience with Jerry, at that moment I decided that I was not only going to make the National Team again, I was going to be the best left back in the world. In fact, I wrote it down on my list of goals that I keep in my shoe bag.

Up to that point in my career, everything had been about attacking. Now I started working hard at the other end of the field, practicing every kind of defensive drill I could find. I had always watched the pros, but now instead of focusing on the great attackers, I started watching world-renowned defenders like Roberto Carlos and Japp Stam. On my team, I zeroed in on Carla Overbeck and Joy Fawcett, in an attempt to create a playing relationship with them and to duplicate their skill in the back.

Making the National Team again was one of my proudest moments, and putting in the effort (doing daily double sessions, most of them on my own—I worked harder than I ever had to make that team) was, with absolute certainly, one of the most satisfying experiences of my career. I don't know if I have become the world's best defender, but I know I attempt to improve, and I've won Olympics gold and silver medals, a World Cup championship, and I'm on my way to the 2004 Olympics—all while playing defense. That tells me I'm going in the right direction. I think that old lumberjack, the one who planned his strategy and sharpened his axe before starting to work, was on to something. I'm not just a believer in Jerry's blue-collar approach, but I guess I'm a red-flannel gal as well.

MAXIMUM EFFORT

I was on my way to the doctor with teammate Joy Fawcett the day they posted the list of the 2004 Olympics Team, but my teammate Heather O'Reilly told me, "You could cut the tension in the locker room with a knife." Emotions ran the gamut, from the thrill of seeing your own name, or a friend's, to the agony of feeling as if your dreams have died. Players celebrated together, cried, and consoled one another. When I got the phone call from Lil (nine excruciating minutes after the list went up), I was thrilled, and relieved, that my name was there. But at the same time, as soon as the realization had a chance to settle in, I was left with the thought that while my efforts were being rewarded, I had also better savor the opportunity I was being given.

The fact remains that achievement is always made sweeter in relation to your effort, while effort itself is most often reflected in how you direct your focus. For example, youth teams are often under the mistaken impression that the longer the time (two hours plus is not uncommon) they practice, the greater the number of training sessions (up to four per week) they have, and the more games they play, the better they get. But professional teams in the United States and around the world often conduct practice no longer than ninety minutes per session, and we never play more than one game per weekend. You can be active without being productive. Focused effort is what produces the goods.

My high school mentor, Bill Hutton, wasn't a soccer guy, per se, but he was a strong influence on my developing focus. He brought his classroom teaching ability to sports. In high school, I was a bit of a whiner, particularly if I was injured or not playing well. And I wasn't very directed in these times. Hutton was also the baseball coach, and one day after school he brought me to work out with the team. What does this have to do with me? I wondered. But he had recognized that I could be much more focused and disciplined, so I began to run and lift weights with the baseball team. I was the only girl, and sometimes I lagged behind fifty yards in the run, but it turned out to be the kick-start I needed to understand serious effort, and to narrow my focus. He had pushed me out of my complacency and taught me to want more from myself.

Even today, I have a coach who is unsparing in his criticism of my 1 v 1 defending. It's a constant source of work for me (drills, games, going up against Cameron or a friend), as well as study (watching games on tape, specifically noticing the timing and subtle strategies of some of the world's defensive masters). I'm going to every length possible to get better.

In sports, like in life, you're forced to accept that sometimes the investment of intense effort pays off, while sometimes it ends in disappointment. The truth is we overcome a lot of negativity in sports (sometimes, maybe, I'm still a whiner). Whether when recovering from injury, or in trying to make a squad, more than one player on this or any other team have heard the words: "You can't cut it." Not allowing anyone to tell you no also spurs effort. But I don't let my motivation become payback: "I'll show them." I make my response self-motivation: "I'll show myself."

I went through an internal battle back when I left Berkeley. Maybe I'm not smart enough, I thought. I'm not as good in class as I am on the field. But I wasn't going to accept the judgment of school counselors or anyone else. I took my education at West Valley and Santa Clara very seriously. I went from a GPA low enough to get me booted out to getting all As and Bs.

Lack of effort is transparent. We see it on the field when someone quits working. But let's not kid ourselves. There are talented people who are successful without putting in great effort. I think that's not worthy, because it isn't living life to the fullest. I get a wonderful sense of pride when I know I've given my all. I felt this way doing double sessions, spending two to three hours a morning—much of it on my own—getting ready to try out for the National Team again, or, even more simply, anytime I'm on the field and I make a really hard run just to draw away the defense, knowing full well I won't be the one on the end of a pass. There's a belief in yourself that comes from working hard. We should emphasize and feed off of our own efforts. This gives us confidence.

In turn, I think that people should have high standards. I think we're all capable of doing more, and once we throw ourselves into an effort, we can embrace the work. Some days, though, I come off the field exhausted, but I haven't necessarily played well. You may work like mad and not perfect a skill, but the training process allows you to see that skill improve down the road. That's why, in this game, effort also requires patience. Effort does not make players better instantly, but effort and time do. Parents and coaches reinforce this by being aware of, and emphasizing, long-term sports development.

EFFORT—YOU GET WHAT YOU GIVE

Life is filled with instances of adults coaxing and hounding young people to work harder, much of it useless or counterproductive. How do we motivate children to want to work on their own? How do we light the fire that makes them appreciate the value of putting in effort? When I made the National Team again, and Cameron made his high school varsity team, it was the result of extended hard work for both of us. What stands out for me was that we each made a personal decision to put forth the effort required.

When I coach children, I never set them up to fail. I try to find ways to make them successful, by giving them reasonable challenges while stretching them a bit outside of their comfort zone, so they experience the results of their efforts. We should seek and create environments that breed success, but not too easy ones filled with false praise either. The point is legitimate praise for legitimate improvement. We should reaffirm the value of effort with honest, positive reinforcement.

I ask a reluctant child to come before the group to demonstrate. You can see his apprehension and embarrassment. He has little confidence. Some members of the group are snickering. But if I am careful, that child will overcome his fear and succeed. And you can see the smile of satisfaction and pride break out on his face. In my own parenting, I constantly affirm Cameron's efforts. He once nutmegged me twice in a game, and he's still talking about it. My way of "praising him" is to let him gloat and enjoy reliving it as often as he likes.

On the other hand, while I'm supportive, I'm very firm about requiring focus. So when I go out to have a kick-around with Cameron and his buddies, I often finish the session by doing something that needs improvement, like work with the left foot. I tell them, "Let's do some shooting." They're all psyched, until I say, "With your left foot." They all moan in chorus, but we share a laugh, and I also focus on having a good time—and on getting some work done.

It's very important to understand that eventually, no matter how young the child, everyone is in charge of his or her own effort. Coaches or parents can request, suggest, or lead, but they can't leap the final hurdle. You can't blame the team, the coach, or the referee if the individual effort isn't there. While a good training session, and the excitement of a game, can feed motivation, there is always that ultimate essential factor: the internal drive to work hard. Our responsibility, however, is to discern the appropriate amount and intensity of the hard work imposed on children. Because we see things through adult eyes, we often don't completely understand or take into account the overall demands put on children in the classroom or on the soccer field.

If you ask me, the physical demands of sports help teach work ethic. You won't find yourself getting any results without effort. I don't mean winning or losing; I mean just getting into the game. Soccer is played on a big field, and at any given time, a player can be involved in the action. But if you aren't hardworking, you'll find the coach unwilling to play you, or when you do get in, you'll hide by not getting meaningfully involved in the action. There's an environment that breeds the combination of physical and mental stamina required to develop a good work ethic. Once you understand that, every area of your life will improve.

WORK RATE

"Work rate" is a term that coaches and players use to describe a player's effort or activity. It's about runs away from the ball (when a player is acting as a decoy or trying to make something happen with an extra attempt to get open), a willingness to fight for every 50/50 ball, and a given player's overall exertion on the field. Most often, a player's work rate shows up late in a game with her willingness to push through fatigue to find space, make runs, and defend. Obviously, the fitter you are, the easier that is. However, you don't have to be the fittest person to have a good work rate. In the end, your work rate is just a reflection of your willingness to try harder. Work rate can also be expressed in your support of your teammates, especially when the situation is tight or difficult. It's a willingness to look outside your position, to take a challenging run or a risk, or to make a run at all. For example, a wide player has made run after run up the side, but hasn't received a pass. Should that player stop running? The player who has a high work rate understands that not every run is rewarded with the ball. While the possibility of receiving the ball is present, the probability differs from game to game. The run should always be made for that *one* time when the ball does come; that player wants to have made the effort to be there. Another component of work rate on the field is concentrated focus. That means constantly evaluating the situation, particularly the immediate moment. It's easy to tune out what's going on if you don't have the ball, or you're not about to receive it. But if you could slow down the action on the field enough, you'd see soccer is like chess. You can't make a move and simply sit back and wait for your turn again. You have to think about the move your opponent is making, how to set up for your next move, and also look three or four moves down the road. Soccer is also about strategy—combinations, subtlety, setting up your teammates, and purposely slowing the pace of the game, making it even more like chess. A player's tactical awareness and sophistication could be confused by the nontrained eye with lack of effort, because he or she is not chasing around all the time. High skill level makes the game look easy, as if the players are putting forth less effort. These players are sophisticated enough to know the time and place for sprinting and tackling. In turn, they let the ball do the work, instead of the body.

Anyone who knows me, or has watched me play, knows that one of my defining characteristics is the wholehearted and purposeful effort I put into my game. It's what I train for, and it is my responsibility to myself, and to my teammates. I take pride in my work rate and am always trying to maximize my efforts on the field. Young, developing players, on the other hand, may not work as hard off the ball because they haven't learned the dynamics of the game. They make a pass and stand back to watch it. This is not necessarily lack of will, just lack of education. It's the job of insightful and experienced coaches to provide that education.

OFF THE BALL

Off-the-ball movement—moving to space to receive passes or open up the field, tracking back on defense, or even shadowing a dangerous attacker as she moves off the ball—is one of the best ways to improve your standing with your team. Even the National Team breaks this down and works on it in various drills. You follow the game with your focus and your feet. Coaches love players who work hard and work smart. So every time you make a pass, no matter what or where, move. This forces members of the defense to alter their positions, and creates new passing and dribbling opportunities.

Truth be told, I didn't always have a good work rate. When things were easy, I was often lazy. But I developed it with good training, an increased understanding of the game, and finally, by undergoing those experiences I outlined earlier in the book when I acquired a deeper sense of commitment and discipline. Eventually I learned that when you're involved in the play, you should try to become more conscious of your work rate off the ball. The game goes up and back, so you should go with it, too.

When I do a clinic with young children, I play a work rate–centered game that depends on constant effort and constant movement. Six players with balls stand in a circle, with one player in the middle. In between the players in the circle are small goals or two cones to simulate a goal or target. The player in the middle receives the ball from one of the players in the circle after he checks off an imaginary defender, passes it through one of the goals, and then immediately turns to receive another pass. The drill repeats this exercise for a set amount of time, going to a different server and goal each time, with the aim of completing a certain number of passes. When done right, the ball and the players are always moving to pass, receive, and shoot. To increase difficulty, you can eventually add defenders.

Even parents can contribute to work rate from the sideline. Instead of joining the chorus of "Boot it" or "Shoot it," or simply cheering a goal, parents can acknowledge hard work off the ball with a "Good run!" or "Way to move to space!" They can also reinforce it off the field by praising players for staying in the game even when the game wasn't near them.

MY BLUE-COLLAR SISTER by Chad Chastain

Celebrity hasn't changed Brandi. She's still just the kid I used to throw dirt clods at. As an older sister, she felt almost compelled to take care of me. But unlike other siblings who fight a lot, we shared a friendship.

The difference between Brandi and other kids was that her work ethic was rare. She knew what she wanted to do, and what she wanted to be, at every point in her life. She recognized it at an early age. You hear a lot of kids say, "I want to be an Olympian, or a World Champion," but they don't really know that. Brandi did. Even when we were kids, I believed her and I felt she could get there, simply because of her ability to play sports—even against boys who were older—and still succeed.

Keep in mind that soccer wasn't a big sport thirty years ago. It was rare to find a girls' league, but Brandi was in one, so we never played on the same soccer team. We did play baseball on the same team, though. Once, Brandi filled in for an injured boy. In that one game, she scored a couple of home runs and pitched a no-hitter. They ended up giving her my spot on the team! It just shows her athletic prowess, even at that age. Still, we were friends.

Back then, there was no system for spotting talent at age ten or eleven like there is now. I think we all fully realized Brandi's true ability when she was sixteen, and got called up to the youth national team. She was more than willing to give up the prom; she wanted to play soccer. My parents and I realized that if there was a place for this game, Brandi was going to be there.

As I sat in the stands of the 1999 Women's World Cup final, I remember my first thought when I saw Brandi was chosen to take the final penalty kick: It's justice. Not that she wasn't given a fair shake, but that this was just the cherry on top of the sundae that she had made for herself. This was going to be her moment, when all the hard work, discipline, desire, and sacrifice she had made over the years to get to this point was all coming together.

Before she took the kick, I buried my head in my hands; a million thoughts were going through my mind. I looked up just as Brandi kicked the ball, and I saw it go into the side of the goal. To be able to step up, especially as a defender, and put it away was amazing. I hugged my parents. Tears of joy were flowing down my face.

Kids in clinics sometimes ask me, "What's Brandi like?" I always to tell them, "You could be like her—a World and Olympic champion. If you enjoy it and you work hard."

chapter thirteen: building the perfect coach

Once after an exhausting training session at Santa Clara, Jerry decided that I needed a little extra work. He felt I wasn't focusing, that I was missing just that extra bit of drive. But that's not what he told me. He insisted that I stay, and asked the goalkeeper to hang around for a "goal-scoring exercise" (and to help frustrate me as much as possible!), because he knows how much I love to score. Jerry set up a drill in which I had to run around a cone and shoot the ball, time and again. "Get it on frame! Choose a better part of your foot!" he shouted. The sun began to set behind the buildings on campus, and by the time I'd made it through one more set of twenty, it was dark on the unlit field.

I'd been at it for forty-five minutes. I was totally spent and was getting mentally beat up by the constant pressure of making split-second decisions triggered by his commands. "Another set of ten," he told me, "You need three good ones to finish off."

Battling the darkness, the goalkeeper (who was having an unbelievable day) and my own fatigue, I struck the final shots, grunting like Monica Seles hitting a backhand. "Now you're getting it," he finally said. Having given it everything I had, I collapsed onto the grass. And that's basically what Jerry wanted: for me to push myself to the edge of my effort, because he knew it'd make me stronger.

Two weeks later, we were in a Santa Clara game at our home field, Buck Shaw Stadium. It was the first time I'd met the U.C. Berkeley squad since transferring colleges, and the game would determine who had the home-field advantage if we were to face each other in the playoffs. With this important implication hanging over us, it turned out to be a difficult game, with a lot of back and forth. It was a very hot night, and, as always, I was sweating buckets. There must have been nearly three thousand fans, all screaming, when I got the ball at midfield, near the touchline. I had a couple of defenders draped over me right away, but I continued to dribble the ball on a diagonal to the far post. I felt as if I was dragging those opponents along, carrying their weight, barely pushing past them. By the time I made it near the goal, there were four or five of them on me. I dribbled into the penalty box on the right side, and drove the ball just the way I had in practice, past the goalkeeper for my second score of the game. I managed to make eye contact with my grandfather, who was jumping up and down in the front row just as my teammates dog-piled on me. The fans streamed down from the bleachers to the railing. Everyone was going crazy.

That taught me yet again how hard training can be a lot like taking medicine. It can seem an unpleasant experience, but it works wonders if you're in the hands of a good doctor. Or, in this case, of a gifted coach.

After the postgame handshakes, Jerry nodded his head at me and raised his eyebrows as if to say, "See, wasn't staying late for that drill worth it after all?" That practice may have been for me as an individual, but it was also for the greater good of the team.

That dramatic goal, one of the favorites of my career, came from that exhausting practice, where my spirit was also developed—the fighting, never-say-die attitude; the knowledge that even if someone tries to push me, I'll find a way to break through. Today, it is that spirit I always strive to take with me into a game, and it's also one that, as a coach, I try to instill in young players every chance I get.

BUILDING THE PERFECT COACH

I've had every kind of coach imaginable: great motivators who were not really good tacticians; decent tacticians who were not great leaders; coaches who were good at the game but had weak people skills; and even the quintessential parent-coach, who didn't really know the game but made it enjoyable for the players and their families. I've had easygoing coaches—the kind who give you one look, and you know they are pleased. Then, I've had those who are intensely verbal and very dramatic.

The bottom line is that whatever the personal style, it's the coach's job to keep an eye on the big picture and to help players to see it as well. A good coach can help his players connect the experience of the sometimes monotonous and exhausting training sessions with the great feeling they have after executing those worked-on skills in a game. In turn, each practice becomes a microcosm of the game. Jerry is one of those coaches who can connect the dots. He knew what he was driving for in that training session in the dark, that the scenario would likely occur in the game. Endlessly repeating different shots on goal would breed the skill and make it accessible, so I would be able to call on it when I needed it, without thinking.

A great coach, however, is much more than just a tactician. One coach in a generation can revolutionize the game through pure strategy and chalkboard Xs and Os. The last person to do that in soccer was Dutch legend Rinus Michels in the 1970s, who, with the help of his legendary star, Johan Cruyff, helped popularize the "total soccer" concept of fluid positions and attacking soccer. Since then there have been small innovations here and there, but the true measure of a great coach is in his ability to motivate and teach his players. And you don't have to be a tactical genius to do that. Personally, I love those coaches who emphasize the fundamental skills of the game and have the ability to encourage and inspire each player on their roster.

In my experience, the best coaches are insightful, inspiring, and compassionate. They deliver a message with clear, sometimes even eloquent language, a calm demeanor, and a sympathetic tone that inspires players to go out and attempt what they're teaching. The skills of a coach and a teacher are pretty much the same, in fact: communicating ideas and concepts so that players or students can understand. They don't just ask players to perform; they set an example, which inspires respect. A great coach can break down the components of the game and put them into simple terms. And when there are problems, good coaches help players to see them, and to find the solutions.

My first season with the San Jose CyberRays didn't start out so well. I felt the weight of responsibility not just of being team captain but also of being one of the league's founding players. Our record was 1–4–1, when I got an invitation from Steve Mariucci, then coach of the San Francisco 49ers, whom I had met at a charity event, to come check out his team's facilities. I felt this was a great opportunity, and perfect timing to get a little inspiration from a highly successful coach, since I was struggling with my own team. Though we play a different kind of football in the WUSA than do the 49ers, Mariucci is the sort of coach I have always respected.

As I entered his office, my jaw dropped as I gazed at all the Super Bowl memorabilia. I sat down and looked across at Coach Mariucci, and suddenly, I burst into tears. Of course, my behavior prompted a perplexed expression on his part. At first, I was so emotional that I couldn't speak. When I finally composed myself and explained why I was so upset, he smiled and said to me in a calm voice I will never forget, "I've coached some incredible athletes, and I said to them the same thing I'm going to tell you now: You play a game for a living, and you can be great at what you do, but there's a limit to what you can control. Do what you can, and stop letting what you can't get in the way." After he finished sympathizing with me, he told me to get myself back on the field, stop worrying, and listen to my coach.

A good coach is also a good listener, since players have concerns or misunderstandings, and they need to be heard. Coach Mariucci went on to explain how quarterback Steve Young had sat exactly where I was, expressing the same doubts about his role as team captain and his leadership capabilities. He wasn't telling me anything new, but he had that way about him—his demeanor, his kind smile, the look in his eyes, and his sympathy— that a great coach has, and I remember the effect he had on me to this day.

I appreciate different styles of coaching, and, in my own coaching, I try to take the best qualities of each, because each one brings something new to the game. Keep in mind, however, that no one coach is perfect, because he can't please all eighteen players, every one of whom wants to be in the top eleven. Not every personality will respond the same way to a particular coaching style, and even those coaches with great traits can fall short occasionally, especially as players mature and squads evolve. When coaching a team, I've found it's best to get over looking for perfection. A coach is never going to have all the answers; he or she should just settle for the wonderful complexity that comes with landing the coach's job.

A good coach can explain a skill, and can also physically demonstrate it. Of course, there are those who learn better orally, and those who need to see visuals. That's something else a coach must realize. It's easy to tell a player having a problem bending a ball to use the inside of the foot and a sweeping motion, but sometimes the light doesn't go on until someone actually shows that person the move.

Of course, it's not a requirement for a good coach to have been a player, but I think it helps. I know Ian Sawyers's coaching is helped by growing up with the game in England, and his time as a player, and when you look at any pro sport, many of the coaches also had decent careers. At the same time, I have plenty of teammates who are incredible players who aren't cut out to coach. Lil loves running her camp, but she admits that finding the patience to work with kids is a challenge. I've discussed it with Kate Markgraf, and she said, "It's just not me." I really like coaching, but I don't know if I'm ready to do it on a high level. I might anger some parents with my honesty!

On the other hand, soccer is just coming into the mainstream in this country, so there's a lot of youth coaches who've never had the chance to play. My father eventually gave it a try, however, and I'm sure it gave him more insight into the sport. He started because he saw how much fun the kids had, and eventually he even took up goalkeeping in a men's league. (I remember his broken collar bone hurting so bad from diving for the ball that he couldn't sleep on his waterbed; he spent ten nights on the couch.) When I was down or hurt, he always encouraged me to battle through it. "Get up, you can do it," was his line. Suddenly, it was my turn. "Get up, Dad, let's go." He'd laugh, and admit, "I see where you're coming from." Though my dad didn't know a lot, he understood that a coach's goal should really be the development of people first, and athletes second. That's something that you don't need a playing career to learn.

I think it's great that Cameron's high school coach likes to get Jerry's opinions on soccer, despite the fact that he has been coaching a lot longer. You might wonder if Jerry is a better coach in terms of knowledge of the game. Perhaps, but Cameron's coach does a great job in asking young players to be responsible for themselves, to be self-disciplined, and to be committed to one another as a team. He has not only instilled in them respect for the team but has also given them pride when they're wearing the school jersey.

We know that, like players, some coaches are better than others, and some just give it their best. The players' job is to place their trust in their coaches and to learn all the coaches have to teach them. And it's the coaches' job to earn that trust and keep that contract, official or unofficial, in mind. It is also the coaches' job to do that without a player fearing retribution. I think this is the most difficult aspect of the player/coach relationship. The coach, usually older and wiser, needs to give the player freedom of expression, creativity, and a sense of personal power. The player should not feel wrapped up in the concern, worrying "Is the coach going to be happy with me?" every time she makes a move can paralyze a player.

FINDING YOUR COACH

People approach me, or Jerry, all the time to ask about finding a coach. "Can you just fire off a few names?" they casually ask. Unlike many professions, almost anyone can become a soccer coach. At the youth level, a lot of times the job is voluntary, and while coaching licenses may be useful indicators for choosing a coach, they often aren't required. More important, there is no test of knowledge, let alone character, you have to pass to get a license. So while Jerry and I know lots of great coaches across the country, we always encourage players and their parents to participate actively in the search. Simply put, you should have a good idea of what you're looking for and do your homework. The younger the player, the more important this research is.

In Cameron's case, Jerry knew Jeff Baicher, the prospective club coach, very well because Jerry had coached him, and Jeff went on to play professionally. I knew Jeff as a peer, since we both attended Santa Clara at the same time. Our experience with Jeff helped make the decision of where to send Cameron very easy. What clinched it was when Jeff said to Jerry that, despite their relationship, Cameron was going to have to earn his position. "We wouldn't want it any other way" was Jerry's response. Then, we knew Jeff was also honorable.

Of course, when evaluating high school soccer programs, you've got to explore the whole experience because school is obviously about more than soccer. (That being said, high school soccer is a way to express school spirit and let adolescents feel a part of something meaningful.) When you're looking for a club program, by contrast, although the social component will always be important, the emphasis is much more on the soccer. So you'll likely want, and expect, more from a club coach than a school coach.

Unfortunately, many take the task of researching a coach far too lightly. But if you have a choice, selecting a coach should be a major undertaking. After all, parents are making the decision to put crucial aspects of their child's development in another person's hands. Choosing a coach is really no different than picking a pediatrician or, in a sense, a psychologist. That's because a coach can have a profound effect on both a child's physical and emotional well-being, including his self-esteem, confidence, and character. That person should reflect not just the skills but the values that parents want their children to uphold.

In the same way you would seek out any professional, search the Internet; speak to other players, parents, and people you respect; and ask for referrals. Find out who is running the show. Is the coach under the directives of a league; if so, what is that league's philosophy and rules? What is his personality, objective, and team philosophy, in training and in competition? Has he played the game? Who are the other players on the team—where are they from, and what is their experience? What color are the uniforms? (Kids want to know!)

If you're a parent, ask the coach to describe his style of communicating to his players (this is very important), to discern whether he speaks freely and respectfully. If you're a player, meet the coach, one on one. How does the coach make you feel? Find out from other players, and their parents, how they feel about listening to the coach during practice and games. Also, is he likable off the field? Do they enjoy his company? Is the connection there?

In the next phase, observe the coach. How is he conducting practice, or coaching a game? In practice, is everyone involved, touching a ball (i.e., not standing around waiting)? Is the coach interacting with players—not just observing on the side with his hands folded? How many players does he reach? Does he make blanket comments, meant for everyone, or specific to just a couple players? He should include as many players as possible.

During games, does he give knowledgeable information—in small doses—from the sidelines? Tone is very important. To yell out to players is fine; to yell at them is not. Since you can't hear his conversation, watch his body language; is it positive? Is he clapping, high-fiving, or patting a player on the back when she goes in or out of the game? How is the player reacting to the coach? Is her head up or down?

Finally, if you don't have choices in your area, you should have an open and honest conversation with the coach and, at the same time, parents should assess the fit by making an honest evaluation of their child—her interests, discipline, commitment, and goals. Whether they're choosing a coach or not, it's their child's future at stake, so it pays to take this homework assignment seriously. As soon as players are of the age to do so, they should also absolutely be involved in the process. Parents should never underestimate their child's impressions and input.

COACHING IN ANY OTHER LANGUAGE

In December 2003, on a trip to England, I met Rio Ferdinand, the central defender for Manchester United and the English National Team, and I asked him about Sir Alex Ferguson. "What do you think of him as a coach?" Ferdinand looked at me as if I were speaking another language.

Ferguson is the manager, he reminded me, to which I explained that, in my country, while not necessarily the case in other sports, at least in soccer we don't usually make that distinction: coach and manager are one and the same. But it's different in most other places. Very often the manager allows the trainer to take training sessions but is fully aware of what is going on, who the players are on a personal level, and how they are performing right through to the youth level. When David Beckham signed on to Manchester United at age thirteen as a trainee, Ferguson knew who he was, who his parents were, who his siblings were, and so on. While he didn't train Beckham back then, he realized when it was time for Beckham to move to the full team, how to use him, and when to give him the captain's armband. Beckham also had the opportunity to sign for Tottenham (his local team), but the then manager of that club didn't really know who Beckham was. So, a thorough manager won out.

In a simplistic way of looking at it, the coach should direct the play; the manager should direct the people. This is particularly relevant in youth sports, because working with children is a specialty.

Since soccer has exploded in popularity in the United States, an entire industry has been built, including professional coaches or trainers, a number of whom have emigrated from other soccer-rich countries. Youth sports are big business, and often when people pay, whether they express it or not, they expect a tangible return on their money. In the quest for a greater understanding of the technical aspects of the sport, perhaps the most underestimated but essential ingredient is the talent the coach has to manage young people. In our zeal to get the highest possible level of education in the sport, we shouldn't be lured into overvaluing someone's technical experience and undervaluing his people skills.

Other professional sports distinguish between the roles of coach and manager. Baseball and football even break it down, with specialty coaches for different aspects of the game, such as defensive and offensive coaches, third-base and pitching coaches. But often, in youth sports such as soccer, the coach is forced to take on all roles.

I think there's a big piece missing from American youth sports. While sometimes you do find a good coach, or a parent or another person steps up to act as a volunteer manager, players and their parents benefit by someone with the skill and the willingness to serve as counselor to the team. We need to start teaching coaches to wear all the hats necessary to do the job well, but also to seek assistance when they need it. It's tough enough to teach the game, let alone to master addressing the personal needs of young players. Most teams have volunteer parent-managers who coordinate travel, budgets, and the innumerable logistical puzzles present in today's youth game. I'm not suggesting every team have both a coach and a manager, like Manchester United, because this ideal may be unrealistic. But I would like to encourage those involved to reevaluate the role and the mission of the coach, and to make a conscious effort to put more emphasis on the people skills of that person.

In an ideal world, coaches should be trained as rigorously, and work just as hard, on how they deliver information and relate to their players as they do on the rudiments of the game. And while I'm the first one to encourage young athletes to be responsive to the coach's suggestions and critique, the same should hold true for coaches. They should maintain lines of communication with players and their families.

Today, I doubt my father could get a job as a youth soccer coach. He didn't have a high-level education in the tactical and technical side of the game. But what he did have—the ability to create enthusiasm and motivate children—was far more important, and he got more out of his players than a lot of more technically sophisticated coaches could. You might question my father's ability to analyze games or come up with sophisticated training sessions, but you would never have questioned his passion for people or his genuine concern for his players. (And I'm not just saying that because he's my dad!)

NOTABLE COACHABLES

Some say that when the pupil is ready, a teacher will appear. When Jerry recruits athletes to Santa Clara, he tells them he's not interested in their technical or tactical background. He considers honing those aspects of their game the easy part of his job. But if those potential student athletes are of tremendous character; if they have been surrounded by people who have taught them valuable life lessons and instilled great character traits; if good people have had a hand in molding them—these are the people he is recruiting, because they will likely be the most "coachable." Coachability describes the willingness of an athlete to be open, and to seek and implement different ideas, techniques, and philosophies.

When the player is ready, in turn, the coach will appear. In the same way we never stop needing practice, we never stop needing a coach. Even though I have played the game all these years, I still need a coach's guidance. On many levels, I believe that a player willing to endure the discomfort and find the humility to work on his weaknesses should have no problem making a lifelong commitment to being coachable, as well.

If we are coachable, we accept our limits and earnestly chip away at the protective shell of our egos, which can keep us from acknowledging our faults. Once we break that down, we can find the ability to understand a concept, and to absorb what the coach is telling us. This isn't just lip service I'm talking about. When I come off the field after a less-than-ideal performance, I ask the coach to "give it to me straight." I vow to be the player who accepts instructions. It's the same in my life outside of soccer. If I am doing a television appearance, I ask the director to help me get it right.

When I was a forward, Jerry used to tell me that when I wanted to drive the ball with power, an instep volley, for example, if I were to rise up—raise my chest, keep my knee above the ball, and generally keep my posture high—it would help keep the ball down, resulting in a more accurate shot. I watched him train Aly Wagner and Leslie Osborne, but I still wasn't completely sure it made sense to me. But when Mia recently asked for advice with her shot, all these years later, out of my mouth came the words, "You need to rise up." She was very open, tried it, and found it helped. She scores more goals than anyone else, so if it's good enough for her, I should do as I say! That's a lesson in its own right.

It's important for players to try to see things from a coach's perspective. I wish I had always been capable of it. Remember, on a typical soccer team, players have seventeen allies, while the coach is on his own. The way I make that clear when I'm coaching is to put kids in charge of teaching the group every once in a while. This shows them what it means to lead, to have people count on them; at the same time, it helps them understand that they have something valuable to offer. Players, I tell people, aren't the only ones who need empathy and sympathy to be great. Trying on the coach's hat also shows them it isn't easy.

It's also vital that parents show support for the coach. Sometimes, we all think we know the answers, and have a better way, but we can't ever truly understand unless we are in the coach's position. When children come to us complaining, we have to be cautious, even if we don't always agree with the coach. Listen carefully, and separate the whining from the genuine gripes. When Cameron complains to me, I tell him, "You know, Bud, you may not agree with the coach, but your team functions under his guidelines. Your choice is pretty simple: Either live by those guidelines and participate. Or don't, and you can watch." Again, this is a tough-love approach, but there are also times when I do agree with Cameron's complaint and then we can still find ways he can live with the situation.

When I played on the San Jose CyberRays in our first championship year, I was at left back. Everything gelled, and we were in sync with one another. In our second year, various injuries created a need to switch me to right back. I was confused and disoriented. I was constantly questioning myself. I couldn't organize my thinking, or position my body in relation to the person behind me. For about three weeks, I simply felt incapable of playing soccer. Everything I did felt wrong. Ian Sawyers, the coach of the team, critiqued me in front of everyone. It didn't feel good, but he had a plan in mind, and eventually, he helped me see that playing on the right side was not fundamentally different than playing on the left. To his credit, Ian was patient. He didn't clog my head with more information. He gave me confidence. After being tough on me—which he was, and I appreciate—he then told me, "You're a good player; you'll get it, don't get in your own way." And I moved on.

Our assistant coach, Tom Sermanni (aka the Silver Fox)—a calm, low-key type who had also coached the women's Australian National Team—was a great balance to Ian. (He was so nonchalant; when I thought he wasn't coaching enough, I used to say to him, "Tommy, can you get on someone?") They let me work things out, even though it took some getting used to. I'd shifted before, and I'll likely shift again, but I bought into the system, and we started winning. I give the two of them most of the credit for our success.

When we join a team and are being coached, we have put ourselves in a situation where we will be analyzed and critiqued. When the coach does this, it can be hurtful. As tough as that can be, it's great when your contributions are acknowledged.

April Heinrichs was the assistant coach of the U.S. National Team for the 1996 Olympics. When I tore my medial collateral ligament (MCL) in the semifinal, she asked me if I could play. I let her know that my leg was hurting badly, and that I didn't want that to be harmful to the team. I asked her advice. "You're better with one leg than most people are with two," she told me. That was a heck of a compliment, and because she expressed it, I felt uplifted. I went out and played the rest of the game with a bum leg and a lot of heart. Coaches take note: You'll get a lot better results balancing criticism with compliments. And players, don't forget: You'll play better if you learn to communicate, and work with your coach. (Note: Sometimes professional athletes play hurt. In many cases, this is a decision made with medical consultation, and weighing benefits and risks. I would never recommend youth athletes play through such an injury.)

PARENTS AND COACHES

It amazes me how many parents feel they have the knowledge, and the right, to question the coach, even in a righteous or belligerent manner. Good coaches train long and hard and often have years of experience. While I appreciate the number of games parents may have watched, that qualifies them to be experienced spectators, not to be coaches. It does not qualify them to make decisions about playing time or tactics.

Parents need to think before they confront the coach. They need to understand that their intense interest and love for their children means they undoubtedly view their sports and games through a very narrow lens. They may have a hard time seeing their child objectively because they have a vested interest.

In the early 1990s, I took on a new job as girl's soccer coach at Monta Vista High School in Cuppertino, California. In the second week of the program, I called a meeting of both players and parents. I wanted them to hear from me, and from one another. Standing in front of the group, I welcomed everyone, and reminded them we had a combination of older and younger players. I went on to say that we were in a good league, and that I had no idea where we would finish in the conference.

Then, I said, "Parents, there are only two rules I have for you. One is to encourage every player on the field, not just your own. Two, if you have any questions, suggestions, or advice, come directly to me. I'd love to have a conversation with you." My message put my sincerity out there: I don't have all the answers, and I'm not infallible; but I'm going to try to play the games with the best interests of the team in mind. If the parents were unhappy on an individual basis, they could come to me and we would work on their concerns. As a coach, I'm going to make mistakes, but this is a great learning opportunity for players, parents, and myself—and if I am not willing to learn from my mistakes, then I am in the wrong place.

Although I had invited input from the parents, ideally the player should be able to come forward and speak up for herself. I know how difficult it can be, but if you are in an environment that encourages open communication, it's more likely to happen. It's up to parents to train their children to express independence. Ultimately, parents shouldn't be the ones to step forward; one day, the players will have no choice but to represent themselves. I know this from experience. My high school coach was a tall, slender, athletic woman who somehow found it beneficial to weigh the players on our team, and to do so in front of the rest of the girls. I had two choices: to find the courage to tell her I didn't feel good when she weighed me, or to internalize it and try not to let it bother me. I never had the courage to make the first choice, but looking back, I wish I had.

WHEN COACHING WORKS, by Tony DiCiccio

What made us successful in 1999? With the pressure on the team to regain World Cup status, the pressure to create something special, and the pressure of the strong possibility a professional league would be created if we could win—the main ingredient for success was how close this team was. This wasn't by accident. We worked on it. They epitomized what a team meant. There were stars from the 1996 Olympics team not starting, and that's a potential cancer, but even they bought into it and felt ownership. They always had one another. They were so close, so connected; that was really the margin of victory for us.

We created a bond by identifying the potential challenges, then my assistant coaches and I worked on it, as well as our fantastic psychologist, Colleen Hacker. We did a lot of team-building exercises.

I also looked at what happened to the Men's National Team in 1998. They imploded and, eventually, pointed fingers at one another in the press. The veteran players on the bench had no connection to those on the field (and their body language showed it). They finished last of thirty-two teams in the World Cup, which was really disappointing because they had the talent to win.

In 1999, many of players were wondering if they were going to start, or how much playing time they would get. At one point, we saw a couple of these players off talking, using each other to commiserate. But they came up to me afterward and said, "We're not going to do a bitching session; we're just going to support and have fun with the rest of the players." The press kept asking me—and Shannon MacMillan, who was playing great—why she wasn't starting. After a couple of games, she came up to me and said, "I know you're getting hammered, and of course, I'd like to play every minute, but whatever you decide, I support." What more can you ask for from a player?

We created a climate, but the players bought into it, particularly the leadership. Every player needs to know her role. They can't be left in limbo. What am I supposed to do? What does he want from me?—those sorts of questions. You have to identify the potential issues, make sure that the players know their role and that, as much as possible, they buy into that role. Then, as a coach, you have to stick to that.

It's a cliché, but it's the players' responsibility to put the team's goals, objectives, and visions above their own. It's not easy. When you talk to a team, they will all agree with that. Now, you have to follow through and deal with that on an individual level, as well. It's not a one-day thing. I had a group of players in '99 that wanted that commitment. They might not always have known it, but what they achieved was the sum of their efforts. That year, China was every bit as good as we were, perhaps a hair better. I don't believe we would have beaten them without that total team commitment.

One of the great challenges with a team like this is I always had to be on the cutting edge of my own coaching. They drove themselves; they challenged me to be that way also. I couldn't be semi-prepared. I had to have a theme for every training session, and a goal, and I had to go quickly from one exercise to the next. It was a great environment for team, player, and coach development as well.

THE BEST OF THE BUNCH

After many years of coaching and being coached, you develop the ability to extract the good, and even make some use of the bad. Your experience on the field also teaches you to enjoy and appreciate the variety of great coaching traits.

My college, national, and professional team coaches have been like snowflakes—no two alike. One that I have enormously enjoyed working with is Tony DiCiccio, best known for being at the helm of the 1999 Women's World Cup, and also as commissioner of the WUSA. Tony wasn't necessarily the supercalm type, but he wasn't a yeller either. He was incredibly open and respectful, going so far as to ask each of us at team meetings to list our favorite lineup. Tony's strength was his commitment to the team as a unit.

For example, no matter how good Michelle Akers was, he didn't put her excellence above anyone else. Whenever there was a press conference, he would defer all credit to the group. "What a great team of players I have to work with," he would brag.

Immediately after we won the 1999 World Cup, Tony came sprinting out to the field with this enormous smile. He jumped up and down, genuinely as excited as a kid on Christmas morning (probably more so). That was the kind of coach he was. He didn't separate himself from the players; he allowed us to see his emotions. Then, right there on the field, he acknowledged the staff with a heartfelt thank-you.

chapter fourteen: you kick like a girl! (if you're lucky)

I was always a tomboy. While other girls played with dolls, I ran around after a soccer ball every afternoon. And it wasn't just soccer that captured my attention. I played on a boy's flag football team in the sixth grade as a starting nose guard. I loved playing, and I never felt as if I shouldn't, or as if I didn't fit in. But some of the adults certainly didn't think that way. Once, when our team went to play another elementary school, my dad overheard another parent (a father, of course) exclaim, "Oh, my God, there's a girl out there!"

A few plays later, when I chased down the opposing quarterback and sacked him, my dad turned to the obnoxious parent and asked, "So, now what do you think?" He mildly replied, "Well, she's pretty good." My dad stood tall with pride and told him, "I know. That's my daughter." The guy patted my dad on the back, smiled, and stayed quiet for the remainder of the game.

You probably expect me to say how much times have changed, but I would only go so far as to say they *are* changing. My regular sessions with Cameron's teams are an example. It amazes me that I can still hear that "whooooo" of surprise and sarcasm from the sidelines when I pull off a move—even though I've had many more years of experience than the boys. And although I'm the first to be picked when they choose sides, that stigma still remains. Among some of the boys themselves it's often no better. One of them will tease, "You just let a girl take it from you!"

On the other hand, when someone makes that comment, I've also heard Cameron, and some of the other boys, step up and tell the offenders, "Yeah, a World and Olympic Champion just stripped you of the ball." Now, if we could just get to the point where I didn't need those titles just to be regarded as an equal player. . . . The fact remains that in every group there will be players and fans who still aren't comfortable with the idea of athletic women and girls.

WE'VE COME A LONG WAY, HAVEN'T WE?

In soccer, I found a great game, but it wasn't always easy to make it my life. When I was growing up, I faced the typical forces working against a serious girl athlete. A big part of what made my career—and many others'—possible is Title IX, legislation enacted in 1972 that created a sea change in women's athletics. Basically, Title IX mandates that benefits be equal to males and females in any educational program that receives direct federal aid. The legislation has particularly impacted women's sports, and it has been credited as a pivotal change in athletics, leading to greater participation and a new generation of female athletes who start their careers younger and with greater expectations and aspirations. But there are still programs not in compliance with the law, and the issue of equality between the sexes remains an everyday battle.

In 2003, Julie Foudy concluded a year's work on the secretary of education's Commission on Opportunity in Athletics, a panel created by the current Bush administration to assess Title IX. Of the fifteen appointees, which included lawyers, professors, longtime college athletics administrators, and a college president, Julie was the only active athlete.

Without Title IX, it's likely neither Julie nor any of the rest of us on the Women's National Team would be where we are. As she explains it, "Title IX is one of the most profound civil rights laws of our time. Striped down to its basics, it means both a son and a daughter have a chance to play sports. If you're using taxpayer money to fund programs, how can you justify 75 percent of every dollar going to boys?" I know that Title IX has directly affected women's soccer. Without it, perhaps the women's U.S. National Team would not have any World Cup trophies or Olympic medals.

THE BATTLE OF THE SEXES

I never had to play coed soccer until I got to Davis Junior High School. And I was never told that I couldn't play until I got there, either. At that school, there was only one soccer team, made up of boys. When I got there as a seventh-grader, no girls had ever gone out for the team. I was among the first few who tried. I went to a preliminary tryout, and, even though it was supposed to be open to everyone, as soon as I arrived, the coach said, "Oh, no, you can't play." It knocked the wind out of me. I felt physically sick and spiritually deflated. Luckily, that's when the boys on the team spoke up. "Why not? She's good," they told the coach.

My lifelong friend Steve Robertson was one of those boys who respected me. Steve, who went on to play on Santa Clara's 1989 NCAA Championship team, says I was one of three dominant players on that team. He later recalled, "I wanted to win, so if Brandi could help us do that, that's all I cared about." He also remembers that the coach never completely accepted me until I became a high school standout. "There were times I felt it was unfair and counterproductive to sub Brandi out of games, but as a thirteen-year-old, I hadn't developed enough strength of will to talk back to a coach," he says.

I played on that team for two years, and while I never considered whether it was good for my soccer development, undoubtedly I got the physical part of my game from experiences like this. Looking back, I can see it was a great test of strength, standing up for what I believed in order to play. I also felt empowered by the boys' support of my ability.

TAKING IT TO THE GUYS, Cindy Parlow

I first started playing with boys at four years old, when my dad was the coach for my older brother's team. That lasted for two years, and then I joined a girls' team by the second grade. But if I had to put my finger on the one thing that made me a better soccer player growing up, it was playing against boys.

I didn't play with boys again until about the tenth grade. My brother played in an adult coed league, and so I would go and hang around, hoping that some of the women on the team couldn't play. I've got two older brothers, Rick, who is five years older, and Joe, who is three years older, and one younger brother, Larry, who is two years younger than me. And I've always played with them. We'd go out on the front lawn and play 1 v 1 or 2 v 2—whatever we had numbers for. I just loved soccer (any opportunity I could find to play I would), and I loved being around my brothers and trying to emulate everything they did. Whenever they went out to the soccer field, I would follow close behind and try to get in any games I could.

The only thing that bothered me was that I was really shy, and to be the only girl around a bunch of guys was nerve-racking. But the guys were great. In my experience, as long as you're willing to compete, and you're good, they welcome you. Later, what I loved most about playing with boys was that I could be completely myself. A lot of times when I played with girls they would get upset if I was too competitive, if I would tackle too hard, or if I was trying too hard. But with the guys it was accepted. They wanted you to go in hard on tackles, to be competitive. I felt a lot more at home with them. I could try to be creative and take them on. It was very important for my development because the guys were usually much stronger and faster, and it was a challenge to find different ways to beat them. I had to be a lot more creative than I did just playing against girls my own age.

That was the great thing about playing in college and on the National Team: I found women just like me. Finding those two teams was like finding my family. I didn't even know there were other girls out there who went through the things I did. If you ask top players in college and on the National Team, most of them played with guys.

My parents also thought playing with boys was great experience for me. Obviously, at first they cringed every time I went into a tackle with a guy. But eventually, they learned I was not made of glass; I wasn't going to break. Then, they always encouraged me, but they never pushed me to do it.

I still play with guys. When I'm home in Chapel Hill, North Carolina, I train with an Under 16–17 boys' team. I was doing that three times a week before I came into the National Camp for 2004 Olympic Training, and I'll start training with them again in the fall, after the Olympics.

I know it's not always easy, but I recommend playing with boys for the serious girl who aspires to go to the highest level. It's probably the best environment to train in if you're at the top of your team and not getting challenged in practices or in games. If you're playing with boys, you're going to be challenged every single time you step on the field. To the extent the guys are faster and stronger, you've got to play a little smarter, find ways to make quicker and cleaner touches.

It's easy for me to say now to forget the social difficulty, but I think that's the main reason why a lot of girls don't try to play with the boys. Attitudes are slowly changing, but when I do camps and clinics I see that, especially at the younger ages, it's still important for the girls to be liked and to make friends. It's hard to get outside of that, to compete and to kick your best friend in the shin if necessary, and for that to be okay. I, too, was shy, and I was initially very reluctant, but after a very short time of playing with boys, I fell in love with it.

MIXING IT UP ON THE FIELD

I'm all for girls playing with boys (I still do it!), but choosing a boy's team is a different consideration. Playing on boys' teams can make girls better players, but there are limits. I think it's a viable choice until about age thirteen; then, the physical size and strength differences make it risky, and it can be a very trying social experience. While girls can gain great skills as players, and there is some social status to be ranked alongside the boys, they will not have the same camaraderie as they do being on a team with other girls. If the boys, with guidance from their parents and coaches, accept the girls they play with as "true teammates," there can be a shared respect and camaraderie, just as girls would get on an all-girls' team. I also think it is a great learning opportunity for boys to share the field with girls, especially in a social context—that is, interaction with teammates, team-first concepts, and communication skills.

I love it when I hear a boy say, "We have a girl on our team, and she's good." It has an impact that extends far beyond the soccer experience. Too often, it's the girls who voluntarily choose to play with the boys, but I like to think of what would happen if things were the other way around.

I did a clinic where two ten-year-old friends of opposite sexes, Meagan and Ritchie, partnered up to do a defending drill. They were having so much fun, I made them my demo pair. They were knocking each other over, joking, and laughing. It never got nasty or one-sided. They were both trying, and succeeding, equally. Usually, when I do a clinic, the boys will complain, "I don't want to go with a girl." In this case, after watching Meagan and Ritchie, the other kids readily paired up. I was gratified to see this small model making a real difference in the attitudes about males and females, and their roles in athletics.

I've spoken to a number of my teammates, and like Cindy, they've related very positive experiences of playing with boys when they were young. It's much rarer today with so many quality girls' leagues, because it's not as necessary, but players who have done it, and their parents, are generally fairly positive about the results—if the experiment is properly conducted. One thing is for certain: Few topics in sports circles get people going like this one. I discovered that when I decided to ask a couple of coaches their opinions.

Ashley Hammond, an Under 14 girls' coach who grew up playing soccer in England, brought his passion for the game to the United States, specifically to Montclair, New Jersey, in 1984. Five years ago, he took a talented and ambitious female player from one of his girls' teams, and coached her for two years on his top-flight Under 13–14 boys' team. (She is currently an All-American who has gone on to be selected for youth national teams, and he credits being on the boys' team as a healthy part of her development.) Based on this experience, Hammond has become a firm believer in mixing the sexes. However, he says, the decision should be based on a keenly insightful evaluation of the players. You need to know the girl, and the boys' team, very well, because, he explains, very few girls can pull it off, and some boys can be problematic. And, too, as he says, "Boy or girl, they have to be good enough to add value to the team."

Hammond points out that great soccer doesn't have to be about physical prowess. "The game always comes down to touch. Carlos Valderrama didn't tackle, and he didn't run fast, but he didn't need to. He was brilliant with his feet and his mind. There wasn't one coach who didn't want him."

Hammond's experience has not been without its challenges. His girls' team once showed up to the field and an opposing boys' team refused to cooperate, choosing to forfeit rather than play. The league forced the boys to play. And in another game, although one boy being marked by a girl asked for her phone number in the middle of a game, Hammond deems the experiment an absolute success, because the girls not only got better, they more often than not beat the boys.

But others believe we are succumbing to a type of political correctness. Bruce Arena, the highly successful men's U.S. National Team coach since 1998, has a different perspective. "How far do you extend this logic?" he asks. "If a girl can play on a boys' team, shouldn't a woman be able to play on a men's team? A woman should not be playing soccer with men at a high level. What is wrong in accepting the fact that there are major physical differences at playing sports at these levels? This is not a demeaning statement." Bruce feels that in our desire to create equality, we may lose a sense of proportion.

"I think the problem is that society today allows some inappropriate situations. Where do you draw a line on what makes sense, and what is safe? Would it make sense for Brandi or Mia to come in to the men's National Team camp? Do we require an equal opportunity clause? Or, do we use common sense?"

How far can women eventually go? Says Hammond, "I'll never utter the word 'never.' Would I like one of my female players to grow up to play in the best environment—on the men's U.S. National Team? Absolutely. Will it happen? Probably not in this century. But if you give up that dream, you give up aspiring to be the best."

LPGA (Ladies Professional Golfers' Association) champion Annika Sorenstam made headlines when she played with the PGA men at Colonial in 2003. She was granted a special exemption to play and failed to make the cut, but people everywhere were rooting for her (and against her). Now, young Michelle Wie has stated her public goal to split her professional career between the men's and the women's tours. When she played at the Sony Open in 2004, she outdrove many of the men and missed the cut by a single stroke. And she's only fourteen! I'll never say never. Maybe there is a Wie out there just lacing up her soccer cleats for the first time.

ROLE PLAYING

I'd like to think I would parent a daughter the same way I do my stepson. In fact, I would hope I would parent her in much the same way as my childhood neighbor Dori Whipple, and my youth soccer assistant coach Carmen Watson, both of whom raised two daughters. They are very loving, involved mothers, but they held their daughters to as high a standard as they would have sons. And that's the same way I feel about coaching. It should be equal.

But it's not. When I coach, I feel the need for a "necessary corrective," because society has lowered the bar for girls when it comes to sports. I think I'm harder on the girls than on the boys; I feel that if I'm not, they may not get the fullest possible sports experience. The expectations for them may be lower, and in turn, they may expect less from themselves.

I want to even the playing field, and to let the girls know that I respect and value them equally—and that's the reason my standards for them are so high. For example, in soccer sometimes you take a knock and hit the dirt. Obviously, I evaluate for injury, but if there is none, I don't let the girls stay down on the ground any longer than the boys. I tell them, "You're okay; shake it off; we need you in the game."

It's like when my grandfather would encourage me with a line from one of the Shirley Temple movies we watched together; he'd say, "Be a tough soldier, Brandi." In terms of the social aspect, I'm compensating. I want girls to be tough, and the boys to be respectful and caring.

The first step is to create an equal environment. When I get out onto the field to practice, I jog, stretch, kick the ball, maybe start a bit of a 4 v 2, but I notice there's a difference between youth girls and boys in this regard. This is a generalization, of course, but the girls like to socialize. They sit around chatting before the start of practice. But when I go to boys' practices with Cameron, even if they're socializing, they're out juggling and kicking the ball.

This might be a case in which the players or the coach set a rule: five minutes of free time, and then it's time to get out of the chitchat mode and into the soccer mode. Or, if they're going to do it, chat while passing the ball or jogging during those prepractice minutes. While I do think a bit of socializing before practice is valuable, there has to be a cutoff, and that is for the coach to decide.

I think it's important that both boys and girls see women play soccer. Most walk away from that experience understanding there are great women athletes, and that knowledge translates to other aspects of life. My objective is to break down some of the social barriers that kept my mother and her generation from the full experience of athletics and, to a degree, even limited me. I want girls to have all the physical, emotional, and social benefits that I see boys enjoying, and to take that into the rest of their lives.

Even my dad, like many coaches I've come across, was different when coaching my brother's high school team than he was when coaching mine. Simply put, he was harder on the boys. It's not that he didn't have high expectations of us girls; he just had a different way of getting through to the boys. I remember asking him why he raised his voice with them. "Because boys don't pay attention," he answered.

Although I'm sure he was right, I happen to believe that they would respond better without the cliché in your face approach. A team's tone is set as soon as a coach takes over the program. He has the power to decide whether he will create an atmosphere of composure and positive reinforcement, built on greater communication, or use the "boot camp" approach, with the assumption that's the only way to get the job done.

Pleasanton, California, youth coach Philippe Blin says the differences lie with the adults, not the kids. "To me, there are no differences in coaching girls and boys. They are both athletes." After thirty years of coaching, he says it's the parents' attitudes that create the gender divide. "They expect a coach to give a female more explanation, or detailed information. They think girls are not as receptive. The parents don't understand that coaches can put the same amount of pressure on a girl. They have the attitude, 'Guys can take it; a girl can't.' These are the old social beliefs, that girls are a little soft."

STEREOTYPES IN THE STANDS

Soccer may potentially be the great equalizer on the field, but off the field, we still face the same stereotypes. Since sports are so physically defined, body image is a relevant topic. I think maybe the reason young people can't get past the sexism and stereotype of body image is because adults can't—particularly the ones in a position of power and influence.

In January 2004, Fédération Internationale de Football Association (FIFA) president Sepp Blatter created a storm of controversy when he recommended women soccer players wear tighter, sexier outfits to bring attention to our sport. These comments irritated me, as well as my teammates, because of the implication that it's necessary to add sex to sell our game, and to promote interest, as opposed to selling the game based on the fact that we're good at it. Besides, it's ludicrous to talk about the size of our shorts, when there are so many bigger battles to fight in women's soccer, such as a global movement to create opportunity in the sport for all young girls.

Still, there are days when it seems as if none of us is immune to the obsession with body image. Even in my National Team household, among professional athletes, we're like many modern women. We have days when we don't feel so great about ourselves. Julie jokes she's "the fat girl in the house." Obviously, that's ridiculous. "Get over it," we tell her.

One of the nicknames my dad used for me when I was growing up was "chunky cheeks." Truth be told, that wasn't a welcome joke. I was a heavy kid, although when I tell people that now they have a hard time believing me. Check out some of my childhood photos in the book. I couldn't hide it! I grew up in a meat-and-potatoes, clean-your-plate household. By the time I was in high school, I weighed 160 pounds. Today, I'm five feet seven inches, and my average weight is 128.

When I was a sophomore, the soccer coach made us stand on a scale, and if you weighed more than a certain amount, you had to do extra running after practice. I was always in that group.

In those days, the soccer outfits were pretty flimsy, with small shorts. (Funny, it's as if Blatter wants to go back in time, instead of forging ahead.) I had to wear two pairs, since they were too small for me otherwise. Luckily, I was a bit oblivious (I was not a reader of fashion magazines), so it didn't destroy me emotionally, but it registered. I never went to the swimming pool with the other kids; I rarely wore a bathing suit, and when I did, I put a T-shirt over it. It wasn't until I was a freshman in college that I got comfortable with my body. These days, we know so much more about nutrition, and especially its relationship to exercise. I never limit what I eat, but I know how to eat right, and to drink plenty of fluids for the amount I work out.

When Blatter's comments came out, my name got tied in because of the shirtless 1999 World Cup photo. I guess I have a history of being connected to the topic. Prior to 1999, I posed for a Nike advertisement about a new material, with the theme that the quality was so good, it made it feel as if you were wearing nothing. The ad showed only my bare back—with no face shot—and my name next to it. Then, there was the more publicized *Gear* magazine photo. It was pitched to me as a pre–World Cup promotion, so I was caught off guard when I realized that they intended for me to pose nude with a soccer ball. Although I was nervous about it at the time, it turned out to be a great experience. Nothing critical was revealed, and the photo was tame enough that it was shown on the *Today* show.

Up to that point, I was quite self-conscious. I still wouldn't put on a bathing suit and go out to the pool. But from that photo shoot, I came to understand that this is who I am, and this is what I'm working with, as the expression goes, and I'm comfortable with myself.

In the final analysis, I want the reason people come to watch to be because they appreciate hardworking athletes and they enjoy soccer—not because of how we look. To do otherwise would not be fair to the thirty million women worldwide who play this game, and just not the right message to the players and parents reading this book.

chapter fifteen: put on your game face

Everything we do on the National Team has a reason, and every ritual has a meaning. The way we prepare for our games is mental as well as physical. That's why our team is famous for the "USA Mentality." While you don't want to get hung up on nonessential details, everything you do in your game preparation can contribute, or undermine, your success. And the greatest example of this I can think of is the 1999 Women's World Cup.

We walked through the shadowy tunnel at Giant's Stadium in New Jersey for the opening game and stepped out into the bright sunlight. A huge roar burst from the capacity crowd. The flashing of thousands of cameras exploded before our eyes, and the smell of the fresh-cut grass was heavy in the air. It was all finally happening.

As I stood there, arm in arm with Kristine Lilly, I was flooded by a rush of anxiety. Oh my God, I have to perform, I realized. I was paralyzed with thoughts I had never had before on a soccer field. What if I can't hold up my end? What if I don't live up to the expectations of my teammates, or myself? I was overwhelmed by the enormity of the game, the culmination of all the planning, training, and waiting. There was even talk that if the U.S. team didn't win the tournament, the event would be a failure and not live up to its promise to prove women's soccer was worthy of attention. I actually began to shake. It must have reverberated, because Joy Fawcett whispered to me, "I'm nervous, too." Whew, I'm not alone, I thought. That helps.

But I was still wound up. My heart ramped up to what felt like thirty beats per second. My blood was pounding. Even with my breathing exercises, I couldn't calm my huffing and puffing. I thought I might have a heart attack during the run in our warm-up routine.

Sports psychologist Colleen Hacker had told us we had to find a way to filter out what we couldn't control. We had to ignore what everyone else wanted—the public, the media—and focus on what we needed to do for ourselves. Even though we were nervous and anxious, Lil and I looked at each other with tears in our eyes. We had done all the right things. We were ready. You don't have to win to make this tournament a success, I thought. All you are responsible for is doing your best, I said to myself then, something I had learned from being involved with the game my whole life.

Regardless of the scale of the event, this same situation plays out on soccer fields everywhere. It's what happens to kids at a big tournament. They get into the game and they're so wound up and afraid of failure, it saps them of all their strength and they can't play. Finding focus at these moments, even for pros, can be a challenge.

Okay. Stop, I thought. I concentrated on the calming exercises we had been doing since Colleen began working with the National Team in 1996. I found my refocusing technique. I bent down and pulled up my socks, one of the gestures we had learned to signify leaving the past moment behind and getting into the new one.

THE 60→30→10 RULE

Before the 2004 Olympics, Colleen did a session with the team in which she discussed the 60→30→10 rule. Colleen explains it this way. "Estimates are that 60 percent of the time, teams or athletes actually defeat themselves by sabotaging their efforts. Thirty percent of the time, the opponent plays at a higher level. Ten percent of the time, the momentum comes during a game—this would be swings in the action, which could go either way, for either team. If a team can control that 60 percent, and add the 10 percent momentum, a whopping 70 percent of the control of the game is on their side!" That's the ratio I was working on in that opening 1999 Women's World Cup game.

One of the most important things that Colleen helps us to remember is that we all have the power to make many choices. No matter the circumstances, we have the ability to focus and maintain a positive attitude. There are so many instances in sports when we can get pulled down, sucked into negativity, defeat, or blame. We rarely come off the field and say we did well; we harp on everything that went wrong. We often let anxiety take over. And although Colleen works hard to help us see the positive, and to use that vision to be winners, we can't count on having someone there to pick up our spirits and get us motivated. We all need to find ways to do that for ourselves.

Of course, a team can still be an incredible support system. It can build you up and give you so much confidence. It can get you through the toughest times. On the National Team everyone who doesn't complete the assigned fitness has to do extra. In our last session, there were two players who didn't get through all of the sprints. A couple of their teammates volunteered to pace them in their extra runs. Aly Wagner was one of them. "I was exhausted from doing ten sprints," she admitted to me, "but I knew those players had only a couple more to do and I wanted to help them. I talked them through it, and because there was no pressure on me, I didn't even feel like I ran!" Isn't it incredible how even the most prepared people can have anxiety, and find it difficult to be calm in tough circumstances? Aly's example is a reminder of how we can do things when the pressure is off and we don't overthink.

You can have all the skill and technique in the world, and your mind can defeat you. You see this happen in sports (and in life) all the time. To be a good player you have to have physical ability; to be a great player, though, you have to have both physical and mental ability.

Looking back at my career, I realize I was once a mental midget. I'd tie myself up in knots with defeatist thoughts, and it would show in my performance. But I've made a lot of progress in turning that around. Just today I faced with terror the thought of doing fitness with the National

Team. I'm recovering from a foot injury, so the mere prospect of jumping back into the toughest part of training is scary. Stop, I told myself in the midst of that negative spiral. You'll be fine. You won't drop out. You need this fitness. Welcome it. That self-talk broke the destructive chain of thoughts. Was the workout hard? Absolutely, but I made it through, and passed. I turned my fear into motivation and satisfaction—what a gratifying experience.

MY WAY, by Mia Hamm

Other than eating my usual pregame peanut-butter-and-jelly sandwich, I don't necessarily have a thought-out pregame ritual. Most of the time I do what's worked for me. I'm pretty quiet when I get ready, and when I'm mentally preparing. I don't know if it's because of the stress of the event, but I'm inwardly intense.

Other people have their own way; some are very vocal or active. The people who get themselves psyched up before a game by being loud or "out there" used to put me off when I was younger, but not so much anymore. If you're really focused, you can maintain your own mind-set. If there's anything that takes me out of my game mentally, it isn't what other people around me are doing, it's me losing my concentration.

Even as a kid I was intense. There were times when I was younger when I wanted to stop playing because I couldn't take it. At ten years old, I sat out a season. But after two weeks, I missed it. Although serious intensity has always been my way, I've actually loosened up a little, even though my teammates would laugh at that notion. True, it's not Julie Foudy—style loosened up. But now, as I approach the 2004 Olympics, I hope I'll be a little more relaxed. My experience of what does or doesn't work has prepared me mentally and emotionally. And this time, I'm going to try to enjoy the event a little bit more than I've been able to in the past.

I think the mental approach you use depends on the type of player you are. I use some imagery, but a lot of my preparation is conserving energy or just focusing on what I need to do. I have a couple of little cues for myself, or technical reminders for when I play, like always going for an aggressive first touch. Not everyone is good with mental imagery or self-talk, though. It's important to find your best form of concentration, but at the same time, you have to have the confidence in your physical preparation. Then, you just reaffirm it with the mental side.

What's great about being on our team is that everyone has a different approach; all our personalities are different. Brandi and I aren't going to prepare the same way, and we probably shouldn't, because we're different people. Kristine will do something different than what Julie or Abby will do. There's no right or wrong. It's nice that not everyone's the same. If they were all like me, the locker room would be like a morgue! In terms of your mental techniques, you have to find what's best for you. There's no one way to do that. We have a sports psychologist, Colleen Hacker, who works with us and gives us a whole array of strategies.

I may be very attentive to detail on the field, but I don't necessarily live the rest of my life that way. There's definitely a difference with my craft. I'm similar to Brandi in the way I approach the game. I like to know how things work: why things do what they do, how to hit a ball with a certain bend on it, reasons for the different ways it moves—that's all very fascinating to me. That attention to detail probably holds true for my relationships. They're like the game; you hope what you put into it is what you get out of it.

I'm extremely sensitive. There are definitely times I get caught up in the intensity I've created for myself. I don't stop to enjoy what's going on. This has happened a lot in my career. But that changes with everything that happens in your life as you get older. I'm so grateful for the many opportunities that have come from my career—not the least of which is finding confidence and personal growth. And that, too, helps the mental part of your game.

TOOLS OF THE TRADE

There are various techniques for "mental fitness," but my personal mainstays are these three: visualization, focus, and goal setting.

Visualization

We do this as a team, and I also do it individually. I learned visualization in college and with the National Team. In both places, we do an exercise to get into a positive frame of mind. Give it a try. Lie down or sit, and close your eyes. Get into a very relaxed state, with no movement. The only mental picture you are allowed is one of yourself doing something successful in your soccer: re-create a good run, a shot on goal, a clearance, or a save if you're a goalkeeper.

See your success over and over again, never allowing a negative thought to enter your mind. Your touches are always perfect, your passes are the correct pace, your shot is always on goal and in the back of the net. When you get into the game and are faced with the same scenario, you'll have already seen yourself complete the task. I see my image in all of its details (the more vivid the picture, the more real it becomes), and I see it in its ideal. For example, I don't just imagine myself passing to another player; I see myself passing perfectly, and to her foot farthest away from the defender. I believe that if I can't close my eyes and see it, it is almost impossible to make it happen. And you need to see it completely and sequentially.

Ultimately, you have to envision a positive outcome. Then, you need the confidence to attempt it; next, you need to believe that you can make it happen (even if it doesn't come off the first time, continue to try), and last, you have to celebrate the fact that you did it. I see all four of these scenarios in my visualization.

Focus

Laserlike focus also gives you confidence and calm. Focus can impact all of your challenges. Pick something important that you want to improve and focus on it—for example, your touch. If you're not confident in your first touch, and it lets you down at times, you won't be able to do the basic soccer requirements.

I'm a defender, and I need to focus on 1 v 1 defending. Now, I could go off and do free-kick training since that is also one of my duties on the team, but I prefer to work on my weaknesses. It's tempting to gravitate to what's easier, and I can find myself doing this. But I know that I need to work on my 1 v 1 defending, so when I can, I will spend my extra time outside of training on this area. That isn't to say that I won't sometimes spend time on other aspects, because I do need to maintain a balance. If you find yourself not going back to the things that should be your greatest focus, there are techniques you can use to help regain a direction.

We all lose focus from time to time, and when we do, it takes us out of the moment. If in any way you lose focus, try these techniques given to us by Colleen Hacker. Give yourself something tangible to do that you have decided signifies refocusing: pull up your socks (if you see us doing this on the National Team, now you'll know why!). Smooth your hair, or pull at the grass. Wear a rubber band on your wrist, and snap it. That's also a good way to defeat self-blame. Snap it, and you signal a stop to the negativity.

Carla Overbeck was the master of focus. She knew when and where to be focused, and exactly what her role was. Her game was not necessarily a physical one, but it didn't have to be. She was so organized and so focused on the action that she saw things early. She got into the right spaces, at the right time. This was part of her greatness. I could always count on Carla not to get rattled.

Goal Setting

I have three types of goals: short-range (also called immediate), midrange, and long-range, and I am religious about setting them and keeping track. I've been setting long-range goals since before I even knew it. I set my sights on the Under 16 National Team when it was just newly formed. "I'm going to make that team," I told my mom before I went to selection camp. And I did. Make the goal real, and you can also make it more accessible.

At about the same age, I saw an NCAA championship game on television for the first time. That's when I realized there was such a thing as college soccer. I decided right then and there that I was going to play in college. My long-range goal became to go to U.C. Berkeley, and I did. The latest long-term goal I achieved was making the Olympic Team. At this point, after having achieved that goal, I now have to create new goals for the Olympic Games—and beyond.

In the meantime, I have learned about how all our goals are related. To become a better player, every day should present a new challenge, physically and mentally, so my immediate goal is what I want to achieve at every day's practice. I pick one aspect from each of the four pillars of the game: technical, tactical, physical, and mental. Sometimes I write them down in my diary. (It's especially good for beginners to do this. I've been making this list since 1996, so on some days, it's good enough for me just to go over the list in my mind.) To create a game goal, I select two to three of the immediate goals from a week's worth of training. One might be: Get into the attack, if I'm playing wide back. Another might be: When I get into the attack, if I can make a cross, reach my target 65 to 75 percent of the time.

Next, I set a midrange goal. It spans a week to a month. Last month I was injured, so my midrange goal was to get healthy and stay fit without stressing my injured foot. Here are the goals I composed in this category, and achieved, covering each of the four pillars: keep fit by riding a bike and lifting weights (physical); focus on improvement by watching players in practice, especially those who will be next to me when I play (tactical); work on a Pelé series of hitting balls with the inside of the foot, thigh, and chest with Joy Fawcett, and heading (technical)—despite being sidelined; stay focused at training, and don't allow my mind to wander elsewhere (mental).

Immediate and midrange goals facilitate long-range goals. You could also call long-range goals your dreams. Making the Olympic Team roster was my dream. Acknowledging it as a goal, and working toward it with immediate and midrange goals, helped to make it a reality. Creating a definitive set of goals makes what is only a wish or a hope—something vague or unreachable—attainable.

To some degree, every professional utilizes mental techniques. Even amateurs adopt them, sometimes just by instinct. I remember when my dad was our youth coach, he would have us lie down on the ground after a workout, close our eyes, and see ourselves in the upcoming game. I doubt he knew he was using this as a sports psychology technique, although the results were the same.

Keeping track of your "mentality homework" also helps you to hold yourself accountable. Once you set goals, you're forced to acknowledge your mission, and that's empowering. Writing them down just reminds you that you've stored them away in your mental "filing cabinet," and that you need to continue to take them out. It also helps you to steer the ship, to know that you are doing what you've set out to do. It's easy just to go through the motions. But most serious players I've known, and serious people, are diligent "list-maker" types. They don't want to miss the details.

Setting goals not only organizes you, it helps take the pressure off. My immediate goals are very simple and doable. I pick small, precise, and attainable feats. (That's why big dreams are reserved for the long-range list.) When I set my goals for the day, it's not a long list. As you attain confidence, you can extend your reach to achieve more goals, but keeping it simple is keeping it attainable.

If you want to fulfill your soccer aspirations (or any aspirations), each of these mental techniques should be a part of your game plan—every bit as much as your physical technique. And you're never too young to start. In the same way you have homework, or chores, you should have your list of "mental homework."

COUNTDOWN TO LIFTOFF

It can be very helpful to create your own ritual, and to stick with it. For example, Cindy Parlow once said she discovered how important her team's pregame meal was when she missed one, ate poorly on her own, and felt weak and tired during the game. Our rituals can be social (team meals are also about team bonding), but personal rituals can also have a physical impact.

As a team, we take it one step further. The night before the game, the coaches give us a talk. We also get a scouting report on the opponent—what their strengths and weaknesses are, and how we're going to attack and defend their team. I soak in the information, and then let go of it. I don't overly focus on the details. The training is already done, so there is nothing more I can do on that front; at some point, you just have to let instinct take over. Everyone needs to prepare in a way that instills calm and confidence, and I think you can sometimes overwhelm yourself with too much information. That's dangerous, particularly if it compromises your ability to have a clear mind, to anticipate the action, and to be intuitive—all essential in the game.

About four hours before game time, we have our pregame meal, usually buffet. The mood during the meal varies from game to game. Sometimes it's quiet; sometimes boisterous; sometimes somewhere in between. After the meal, we have about an hour to get prepared. Some people begin their preparation before we leave the dining area. I go over my gear. I always like to get my bag and cleats ready. I make sure I have my shoes shined, and a full second set of clothes. (Because I sweat so much, I change at half time.)

We then board the bus to the stadium. We are always at the game field an hour and three-quarters to two hours beforehand. This gives us plenty of time (nothing defeats a team like being late, and having to miss or rush preparation). During our warm-up, I use self-talk, which I also use throughout the game, as a focusing technique. That self-talk is always positive. I evaluate my touch during the warm-up, and perhaps make a few adjustments, or hit a few balls and correct my strike if necessary. But I never say to myself, or to anyone, Oh, I hit that one bad. Or, That was terrible. Instead, I go back to visualization, and see a time when I hit a really good ball in the same situation.

There have been games in which this kind of self-talk has really saved me—such as in the 1999 World Cup final against China. I was so exhausted, physically and mentally, that I talked myself through the entire last fifteen minutes of the double overtime. I put great faith in the idea that my body would do what my brain told it to do. I hit that PK just the way I told myself I would. It was a direct translation from will to reality.

WHEN THE WHISTLE BLOWS

In our first game against Denmark in the 1999 World Cup, I hit a long ball from my left back position to the opposite side of the field, where Mia collected it, took on a player, and scored the first goal. I knew we were going to take over.

From that moment, we didn't let Denmark get into the game. This became critical to our moving forward in the tournament. It was our "coming-out" party, so to speak. Everyone had talked about the success of the tournament, and if we didn't have a good first game, it would have left the door open for someone else to gain confidence. We came out with guns blazing, with the sole purpose of making our mark.

Every time you start a game strong, it inflates your confidence and puts the opponent on their heels. And, too, it was important that Mia scored. That's why they say: As go your goal scorers, so goes your game. Of course, your team has to be deeper than just good forwards, but you can't win without someone scoring.

That kind of momentum swings both ways, however. We recently played Japan, and they scored first. Here we were, down to them— another 2004 Olympic Team—yet one that had not finished even in the top five in any international event. Obviously, just getting that goal boosted their confidence, and could have deflated ours, but our team's ability to fight for the full ninety minutes is what makes it so difficult for our opponents. They are under constant pressure because we are a team that just doesn't give up. We battled back and the game ended in a 1–1 stalemate.

No matter what happens early on, remember that the game is ninety minutes long—and a goal can be scored in the blink of an eye. At any point, your momentum can change. No matter what happens in any game, I try to maintain the confidence that we're going to win. Our team has a quiet confidence. You don't have to be cheerleaders, with the "We're so good, we're going to kill 'em" attitude, to get psyched up. In fact, I think if you do too much cheering, you're not focusing.

In the 1999 World Cup quarterfinals, we came back twice against Germany, and eventually won. That was persistence, and knowing we were prepared. We had gone through every scenario so many times in training that when this one came along, we were ready to meet it.

How do you decide what's the right mental technique for you? As Mia points out, different people respond to different approaches. It's up to the coach to find what tone works for the group. He has to blend what he likes—his personal style—with what he feels the majority of his players need. In terms of individual attitude, I tell kids all the time that they have to find the confidence within themselves. I don't go beating my chest, roaring, "I'm the best." But I believe in myself, and believe that I'm capable. I tell myself I wouldn't be in the game if I weren't. I try to keep the same mind-set, and use the same mental techniques, whether I'm playing a scrimmage against a younger team, or playing a major final against Germany or China. If I don't do that, if I let down in my mentality, I may not be prepared for the ultimate goal: like playing in the Olympics. Mentally as well as physically, it is important to keep your standards high. That's how all of us get better.

DEFEATING DISTRACTIONS

You need a rock-solid mentality once you get into the game. Stressful distractions can naturally happen in the course of playing. You must find ways to deal with them and keep your focus. Practice this in training, and translate it to the game. Try finding your own techniques to get your focus from the beginning—like deciding the minute you tie your cleats that you will shift solely into the playing mode. Then, stay that way.

I'm an emotional player who gets caught up in what I do. Obviously, that can be good and bad. If you're like me, you'll encounter tense moments. Try to deflate the situation. Sometimes I laugh or smile when things go wrong. It helps me not to get angry, or too worked up. Maybe I exchange a quick few words with my teammates, so I take the focus off my tension with the opponent (or the ref!).

My advice to players: Put on your game face. Don't get rattled. There are scores of techniques to keep your cool, and to keep you focused. I look to Joy Fawcett as a perfect example. When someone nutmegs her, which can be embarrassing enough to throw anyone off her game, she just works harder, as if to say: "You think you've got me, but you don't. It's not going to bother me. You may have gotten the ball past me, but you're not going get it through on the other side." No matter what her opponent pulls on her, she's still determined.

Sometimes, you need just as much focus when you're on the side-line. Being on the bench, whether it's because of injury or because you're a sub, you should still stay part of the game. You're not playing; ask your-self, what are you going to do now? You have to find a way to gain some-thing for yourself, and to contribute productively, and that happens first in your head. Use self-talk to help you focus on reading the game or go stand near the coaches, both of which are more active rather than passive tactics. Be prepared for the moment you do get into the game. When you get subbed in, you won't waste time trying to find your focus on the field.

Just being in the soccer environment has always automatically made me focus. But sometimes, you have to fight distractions, and some-times, you just have to let those thoughts in, get over them, and move on. If you try to pretend they don't exist, and that they're not that important, they can just become heavier. When I was younger, I would still think about the outside world, such as stressful homework, and I would become obsessed. But eventually I learned that by accepting there are distractions, and that you may not be able to control them, you can often let them go.

In fact, the soccer field can be a great place to diffuse life's distrac-tions, a refuge where you get away from problems. That's how it's always been for Kristine Lilly. "Growing up, the distractions were kind of a moti-vation for me," she says. "When things and feelings were crazy in my life, like they are for a lot of young kids, I dealt with them better, and played better, when I was able to release myself on the field. I remember the peer pressure. I was a tomboy. I wasn't the one liked by all the boys, and that hurt sometimes. But it's not as bad if you're doing something you love. The field has always given me a place to feel comfortable. I let everything out there. Growing up, if I was angry, or sad, I let the ball take it away. As an adult, I'm better at handling my feelings, but the field is still a great refuge for me."

PASS IT ON

Before the 1996 Olympics, the Women's National Team sports psychologist Colleen Hacker started a tradition. She would put inspirational notes under our door, and hang quotes up in the locker room before each game. Here are a sample of two that I've kept from that time; they continue to speak to me:

> *What lies behind us and what lies before us are tiny matters*
> *compared to what lies within us.*
> —EMERSON

> *We rise to great heights by a winding staircase.*
> —FRANCIS BACON

Your call to action is to come up with some inspirational words (or pictures) for you and your team. They don't have to be famous; they can be from family, friends, or coaches, or even something you read in a book. Put them up on your walls, or hang them on your refrigerator—anywhere you can see them a lot. Or, surprise your teammates by passing them out before an important game.

epilogue: the me i want to be

When Gloria asked my teammates (and current housemates) what I'm all about, Lil said I'm free-spirited and
I love life. Mia said I go into everything with my whole
heart. And Julie said she sees so much of my mother,
Lark, in me, because my mom was so thoughtful, and because she used
to light up a room when she walked into it. Yep. I'm positive and sunny.
But the sun doesn't always shine. When they answered Gloria's questions,
they were really talking about the best parts of me, the me I wish I could
always be

I love my game, but for a brief time last year—and for the first time
in my life—I lost that love. In the winter of 2003, less than a year after my
parents died within seven months of each other, the grief and loss finally
hit me. I was utterly depressed. I couldn't get myself out of bed, and when
I did, sometimes I didn't even change my clothes. The National Team was
about to take a trip to China, but the last thing I wanted to do was go onto
the field. That's where I had always found my comfort and my strength, but
during this dark time, I couldn't even muster the energy to kick a ball. Physically and mentally, I just didn't feel ready to leave home.

Up to that point, I suppose I hadn't let myself truly grieve. There
were always so many distractions, and the need to keep up my public image of strength. I got to the World Cup, and when I got hurt, I felt the sting

of that longing to pick up the phone and call my mom and dad. The holidays came, and I faced my first Christmas without them.

It took me a rough couple of months to climb out of the grief. And not surprisingly, if you've read the book, a lot of what helped get me back to myself, besides the incredible love and care of my husband, Jerry, were "the girls," my beloved teammates. They were my support system. Along with Jerry, they helped me to rediscover the game I love, and to laugh again. All the reasons I have raved about them in this book were so apparent to me in my darkest hour.

I wrote this book, I realize, because I never want to lose sight of what this game has given me. I want to bask in this gratitude, and to let that appreciation always remain alive in me.

In the months leading up to the 2004 Olympics, when we weren't training with gut-busting intensity, I was sewing a skirt. Now, you should know, I'm very new to sewing. I've never made a skirt, so I was at it for hours, trying to figure it out. But it's worth it. It's a gift for our National Team trainer, Debbie Prose. We have a skilled group of trainers, and I appreciate them all—Cody Malley and Julie O'Connell included—but lately, in their absence, Deb had to take on the responsibility full time.

She has worked so hard to help me rehab my injured foot. She massages it and does manual resistance before and during practice, if I'm sidelined. She'll stay after training to make sure I get whatever I need, like my orthotics, and she even makes my doctor's appointments. And she's not getting paid overtime for any of this. (No one on this team could ever be paid enough to indulge us in all our aches and pains!) Sometimes, we too easily forget those people who make our opportunities possible. Losing my parents has taught me to remember that. So, sewing this skirt for Debbie is my way of saying "thank you." It's an example of my continuing appreciation for the kind of people who get me where I am. (Don't worry, Julie and Cody, in due time you'll get your personally sewed gifts from me, or something else by which to remember our Olympic experience.)

The enduring aspect of what I have learned is that every interaction I have with someone, whether it's on the street or in a stadium, affects me. It either reaffirms or changes my perspective. All of these encounters help form who I am. My way of being involved in life is to be involved with people.

It's the same for me with the game of soccer, and that's why I can't imagine ever letting it go again. But I'm not sure that's what those on the outside have in mind. Lately, I'm hearing a lot of talk about this being the last major event for the veteran players, including me. I'm not saying it isn't; I'm just saying that I'd like to run the race before I think about the finish line. Several of my longtime teammates (Mia, Julie, and Joy) have talked publicly about moving on to something else after these Olympics. I just try to focus on the time we have left together on the team. Although I must admit, I do like Julie's plan for her own retirement: "I'm a sun chaser. I'm going to sit on the beach and have drinks with a lot of umbrellas in them."

In the meantime, I'm a believer in living in the moment. That's what I did in the 2004 Olympics in Greece. We passed on the drinks with umbrellas, but from the kid goat and Greek potato pie in the twenty-four hour cafeteria to the courtesy haircuts, my teammates and I savored every minute of those Games. We spent a month enjoying life in the athletes' village, as large and lively as a small city—which just happened to be populated by the fittest people on earth.

Always the soccer nut, one of my favorite moments was meeting and swapping jerseys with some of the best players in the world. And it was flattering and gratifying when athletes from other countries or sports recognized the veterans on our team and asked if they could get pictures with us. Not so long ago, we were the ones asking for photos. Even though this was my third time around and our circumstances were very different from 1996, this Olympic experience was as powerful as my first.

But it was also an incredibly difficult test for me. Up until our quarterfinal match against Japan, I didn't play a single minute—three games spent entirely on the bench. And I'll admit I struggled mightily with my emotions. But my first responsibility was to cheer and support my teammates, to stay strong, mentally and physically, and be ready when called upon. So, no matter what I allowed myself to feel and express in the privacy of my room, when I joined my team, I put that pain and frustration aside.

When the coaches called me in for a meeting before the quarterfinal and informed me I was starting, it was a total reversal—from near despair to complete elation. But I didn't want to be put on the field out of loyalty or because of pressure from the media. So I took a deep breath and told them, "I want the decision you make to be for the good of the team." Thankfully, my starting spot was confirmed. I then had to contain my emotions and keep the news from my teammates until they had their own meetings with the coaching staff.

Before the game, Lil and I observed our usual ritual: We slap hands or touch knuckles, and say together, "Here we go!" When the starting whistle blew, I reminded myself to stay calm and keep it simple. I played for the full ninety minutes in our 2–1 victory. When a reporter asked me how it felt to be back on the field, my response was simple: "Terrific." I was happy for myself, but even happier for the team. And I was just as thrilled to be on the field in our nail-biting semifinal game against Germany, which in my opinion ranks among the most exciting women's games ever played. The Germans had eliminated us in overtime of the 2003 World Cup semifinals and looked as if they might repeat history when they scored in injury time to send the game into extra periods. But Heather O'Reilly netted a dramatic overtime winner off an assist from Mia, and we held on for a 2–1 double-overtime victory.

As intense as that game was, the drama and emotion were even greater in our final game against Brazil. It started pregame in the locker room, where the entire team hung up all of our jerseys in a symbolic gesture of our shared history. As we took photographs together, there was a palpable sense of nostalgia, and also excitement. After more than fifteen years, we were about to take the field together for the last time.

As overwhelming as these moments were, when it came to the game, I felt fresh, calm, and in control out on the field. Although only two yellow cards were given, the game featured an astounding forty-seven fouls, as both sides came out ready to do whatever it took. But I was careful to keep my feelings in check. "If you let them see they are getting into your head," I told myself, "they raise their emotional level and use it against you." That didn't stop me from expressing my enthusiasm, though. After Bri made a great save, we spontaneously bumped chests like a pair of wrestlers.

When I was subbed out in the sixtieth minute, I wasn't ready to go, but I knew Cat Reddick and the team would take care of business. Age was not a factor. Just as we had said to the younger players earlier, "The ball doesn't know the age of the player kicking it," we now told them to go out with confidence, and to do a great job. So I settled in next to Cindy Parlow at the end of the bench, and we acted like, well, like my mom did on the sidelines of my youth games, minus the megaphone. Through another double overtime, I watched as my teammates gutted it out against the incredibly skillful Brazilians, and in the twenty-second minute of overtime, Abby Wambach skied above the Brazilian defense and met Lil's perfect corner kick with a twisting header that found the back of the net. The '91ers had officially passed the torch, as well as the ball.

When the final whistle blew, it was time to laugh, cry, and scream for joy. On the medal podium, I stood with my old teammates as we belted out the national anthem through smiles and a few tears. (Reacting to our vocal talents, Bob Costas would later remark in a postgame interview: "I'm pretty sure that's not what Francis Scott Key intended.")

Back in the locker room, everyone made a big circle. Julie thanked the staff, trainers, and equipment managers—all those people who can't sit on the bench and are often overlooked. And Bri made a speech about her late father: "Thank you all. That flag waving was for my dad. I felt him looking down on me." I had the same feeling. When I gave Jerry a big hug and kiss after the game, he said, "Your mom and dad are watching. You should be so proud."

By the time postgame interviews were over, it was 3:30 in the morning, and I had all of two hours to sleep before being awakened for drug testing at six. We saw a bit more of the Olympics, but I couldn't wait to get back home, to my own bed, to walk my dogs, ride my bike to Jerry's office, and get back to training at the familiar fields at Santa Clara.

Of course, after the Games, people wondered if, like my friends, I was ready for the lawn chair. Well, a while back, I set myself a goal of two hundred caps (international games) to join the exalted company of my friends who have reached that landmark: Mia, Lil, Julie, and Joy. That means I'd have to keep at it at least into 2005. I won't stake the success of my career on whether I hit that number. But if I do, it will be a symbol of the perseverance and dedication that have carried me through my career and my life.

When you start something as big as a book, you can't imagine the ending. It's that way in my career, too. But, at least for now, I'm at my final words here. Even though I have reached the end of the book (and maybe the end of my playing career), I will always remain on the journey of learning and growth. And whether I become a coach, or a new mom, or go for three hundred caps, soccer will always be a part of that.

appendix: giving back

Here are some suggestions, but feel free to find your own opportunities to give back. After all, they're everywhere.

Children's Cancer Research Fund

www.ccrf.org—A California-based charity organization committed to funding innovative and progressive research in the fight against childhood cancer.

The Taylor Family Foundation

www.ttff.org—An organization that raises funds to serve children suffering from HIV / AIDS and other life-threatening diseases and disabilities in northern California. Camp Arroyo is a beautifully designed, environmentally friendly facility located in Livermore, California, and is used as a Summer Youth Camp by these children. To contribute funds, or even to attend camp and work as a youth volunteer (ages sixteen and up, room and board included, with or without a parent; age fourteen and up locally), contact June Johnstone, Executive Director, The Taylor Family Foundation, 925-455-5118 (phone), 925-455-5008 (fax), kids@ttff.org.

Silicon Valley Children's Hospital Foundation

www.svch.org—I'm on the board of directors of this foundation. Its affiliate is Soccer for Hope.

Soccer for Hope

www.soccerforhope.org—A group for children with life-threatening diseases, this organization sponsors soccer camps and other activities. Check on the Web site for ways to get involved.

Ponytail Posse

www.ponytailposse.com—The official fan club of the U.S. Women's National Soccer Team Players' Association, providing fans with the opportunity to connect with the U.S. players. See United Soccer Athletes for the charitable connection.

United Soccer Athletes

www.unitedsoccerathletes.com—The U.S. Women's National Soccer Team Players' Association charity of choice is the Women's Sports Foundation. Portions of proceeds from certain product sales, auctions, and special events that the players are involved in go to the Foundation.

America Scores

www.americascores.org—The nation's only inner-city after-school program that uses soccer to inspire health and literacy among urban public school students. To get involved as a referee or assistant coach, or to organize tournaments and events for the students, go to the Web site and find a Scores program in your area.

Below are programs of two major youth soccer organizations that feature charity and community service:

American Youth Soccer Organization (AYSO)
(800) USA-AYSO

> **www.soccer.org**—Through this all-volunteer organization, learn how to be a coach, referee, or work as an AYSO volunteer or VIP BUDDY (able-bodied persons helping disabled people play the game). Also, check out CAP, which promotes community service, and look into scholarship opportunities for AYSO volunteers. Go on the AYSO Web site and click on "National Regions" and find your local region.

U.S. Youth Soccer Association (USYSA)
(800) 4 SOCCER

> **www.youthsoccer.org**—Relevant programs are TOPSoccer, Kicks Against Cancer, and Soccer Start. Beginning in late 2004–05, a mentoring program will be started for elite players to serve as coaches and role models by working with recreational soccer clubs.